Motivation Is An Inside Job

Motivation Is An Inside Job

How to really get your employees to deliver the results you need

Norm Crouse

iUniverse, Inc.

New York Lincoln Shanghai

Motivation Is An Inside Job
How to really get your employees to deliver the results you need

iUniverse books may be ordered through booksellers or by contacting:

iUniverse
2021 Pine Lake Road, Suite 100
Lincoln, NE 68512
www.iuniverse.com
1-800-Authors (1-800-288-4677)

ISBN: 0-595-33948-4

Printed in the United States of America

Contents

Introduction

The first person I told that I was writing a book was a good friend who asked me a very direct question: "Why would you write a book about that?" That is a question on a potential reader's mind as they first consider if they will read a book or not. The other two questions my friend did not ask but are on a potential reader's mind are "Why should I read your book?" and "What makes you qualified to write this book?" So I'll begin by trying to answer those three basic questions.

Why this Book Was Written

Most managers struggle every day with how to motivate some or all of the employees they manage. After 30 years in the business world, the last 15 of which I have spent helping managers develop more effective skills; I have a clear picture of the problems facing those managing employees. I am more convinced than ever that the problem of how to better motivate his or her direct reports is the most significant challenge for every manager. Most top executives are aware of the challenge and invest substantial money in bonuses, incentive plans, stock-options, and training and motivational programs trying to address it. That concern cascades down to front-line and middle managers who also feel the pressure of the motivational challenge. They are frustrated because they are not satisfied with the answers they have about what to do about it.

Problem One: Theory Doesn't Go Far Enough

So why do managers face such a difficult challenge in trying to motivate their employees? There are three contributing factors to this problem. First, the motivational research is conducted by academics. I don't have any grudge against professors and research psychologists. In fact, I am sure that they have contributed significantly to our understanding of motivation over the years. For most managers trying to motivate someone who reports to them, the theory is interesting, but it doesn't give them the practical tools and skills they need to apply the theory in the real world. In some cases the theories address factors that are, for the most part, beyond a manager's direct control. For instance, most managers have little direct control over salaries and benefit programs. Other motivational theories address factors within the manager's direct control, but the manager doesn't know how to apply the theory to create behavioral change. While coaching one manager, he put this problem very directly. After reading about Victor Vroom's Expectancy Theory, he turned to me and asked "But what do I say to Sally tomorrow? How do I use this?" So I wrote this book to provide an answer to that manager's question about how to translate theory into management actions to motivate Sally.

Problem Two: Lack of Training in How to Motivate Employees

The second contributing factor to the challenge of how to motivate an employee is the fact that our business schools aren't doing a very good job of preparing managers to manage. Professor Henry Mintzberg, in his book *Managers Not MBAs* cites a Business Week survey (March 24, 1986 pg. 63) titled "How Executives Rate a B-School Education." One of the key findings of that study was that 86% of the top executives surveyed agreed with the statement "Business Schools teach students a lot about management theory but not much about what it takes to run a company." Of course, a key competency in running a company is how to motivate the employees you manage. So, I wrote this book to provide a toolbox to help managers more effectively motivate their employees.

Problem Three: A Changing Work Ethic

The third contributing factor is that the expectations of the workforce are changing. I facilitate management workshops all over the United States, training more than 1,000 managers a year from many different organizations and a wide range of businesses. It is almost impossible to complete one of those workshops without having several of the managers get into a conversation about the changing work ethic of today's workers. Of course, their observation is that the work ethic is deteriorating and that it is becoming increasingly difficult to motivate performance.

The most dramatic evidence of this shift that I am aware of is the work that the Gallup organization has done on employee engagement. I first became aware of this work in a April 16, 2001 article in InfoWorld titled "How to Engage the Disengaged Worker." The article quoted data from a Gallup poll that showed that 19% of the workers surveyed reported being actively disengaged. Another 55% reported that they were disengaged. The figures so shocked me that I started digging into how the survey was conducted and how it measured disengagement.

Basically, actively disengaged means that an employee is motivated to slow business down and deliberately undermine the organization's effort to deliver productivity and quality to its customers. Disengaged means simply that the worker is doing the minimum amount necessary to keep from getting fired. In other words the vast majority of the workforce (19% + 55% = 74%) is not motivated to fully contribute what they can to an organization's effort to deliver results! Gallup's work completely floored me and I have watched with interest as they have expanded and updated their data on worker engagement. If you want to follow their work, do a Google Search on the phrase *employee engagement*. The more I learned about this trend and heard from the managers in my workshops, the more I realized that managers needed more definite guidance on how to motivate employees. So I wrote this book to distill fifteen years of consulting and coaching experience into a roadmap that a manager could follow to deal with an employee motivation problem.

Why You Should Read This Book

The second question to answer is why you should invest your time and money to buy and read this book. The target audience for this book is managers at all levels in an organization that have employees that report to them. So, to bene-fit from this book you must already be, or hope at some point in the future to be, a manager in an organization. If you fit into the target audience, there are three primary reasons to read this book.

It Provides a Useable Framework

Like most complex challenges, the framework for addressing motivation prob-lems is deceptively simple. First, a manager must figure out what they mean by motivation. So the book builds a framework for working with motivation by defining exactly what a manager is trying to manage. This definition of moti-vation may surprise you because it excludes one of the major factors that man-agement has focused on in the past—money. The framework also provides a way to effectively diagnose the nature of the employee's motivation problem. This allows a manager to answer the basic question "What's really going on with this person?" Using only two factors (Perceived Value to the Employee and Locus of Control), a manager is able to quickly analyze and properly diag-nose the factors influencing an employee's motivation.

It Provides Easy to Use Tools and Guides

Next, the manager needs some tools and guides that help them apply the framework in their day-to-day work world. They have to have choices from which to build customized solutions. As I work as a business coach with man-agers, I see that their frustration level is inversely related to the number of tools that they have available to work on a problem. They feel stuck if the tool they are using now is not working and they don't have another tool to use to try to solve the problem. In this book, you will learn four guides and four spe-cific tools that you can apply to employee motivation problems. Then you will learn how to use each through detailed examples. Those examples are the third reason you should read the book.

It Provides Specific Examples

For each of the tools, you will see a specific example of how to use that tool with an employee. The examples show actual dialogue that occurred between a manager and an employee using the tool to solve a motivation problem.

From my experience with management training workshops, I know it is important for managers to have these kind of real-world examples.

The Author's Qualifications to Write This Book

Just because an individual can identify a problem like the challenge a manager faces in motivating employees doesn't mean that person can (or should) write a book about how to solve that problem. So what makes me qualified to write this book? To answer this, I have to look back at my own struggle as a manager and how I went about solving this problem for myself. When I was first put in a management position, I just assumed people would follow me because I was given the organizational power of the role. That naive notion was short-lived. Once I was humbled by a healthy dose of reality I was still faced with the job of motivating my workforce. So I went back to school.

Education

So the first reason I am qualified to write about motivation is that I have studied the topic in a great many venues. As a small business owner, I took several of the American Management Association courses on Management. I studied self-image psychology with Lou Tice at The Pacific Institute in Seattle. I took graduate level business courses at two different universities and completed my MBA. I'd like to say the formal classroom education was enough, but it wasn't.

My mother was an avid reader and always use to say to me, "If you can read, you can do anything." While I didn't always follow Mom's guidance or advice, for some reason this stuck with me. So when I found my formal schooling insufficient to help me attack the employee motivation problems, I started an extensive self-directed reading program to learn what others thought about how to handle the challenge. I wanted to know what those who had come before me had done about the problem. So I read extensively from the works of folks like Abraham Maslow, Douglas McGregor, Frederick Taylor, and Elton Mayo. I also started attending workshops held by motivational speakers like Zig Zigler, Tony Robbins, and Tom Hopkins. I purchased and read books on organizational development such as the *Annual Handbook for*

Group Facilitators from University Associates. I maintain a discipline of keeping up with the field through journals, regularly reading business publications like Harvard Business Review, Business Week, Fortune, Forbes, Fast Company, Inc, Business 2.0, and Psychology Today.

My consulting and training work takes me all over the United States which means I spend a lot of time in airplanes. The advantage of that is that I have a lot of time to read. So I am able to keep up with the heavy flow of business oriented books that are published each year. The constant discipline of immersing myself in books like Jim Collins' *Good to Great* and Howard Gardner's *Changing Minds* has sharpened and focused my thinking about motivation.

In addition, I invest heavily in attending management workshops from leading organizations such as Kepner-Tregoe, The Center for Leadership Studies, George Washington University, and Harvard University. This not only keeps me informed about what others are learning about management, it forces me to constantly review and sharpen my own approach.

Training and Coaching

My consulting practice is focused on four specific areas: process improvement, executive coaching, management training, and facilitating management retreats. All of this work has provided me with a rich environment to develop and test the motivational framework, tools, and guides presented in this book. In the fifteen years I've been involved with organizational development work, I have had the privilege to work with many managers and their employees. That experience has allowed me to develop, test, and refine what I present here and to hone it down into a practical, no-nonsense approach. What you'll read in the following pages isn't just some good idea, but tested and proven tools and approaches. So if you have some employee motivation challenges you need to address, turn the page and let's get started.

Summary Three Questions Readers Ask

Why *Motivation Is An Inside Job* **was written**

- Theory doesn't go far enough in helping managers motivate employees
- Management training is inadequate to teach managers how to motive employees
- A changing work ethic is creating increasingly difficult employee motivation challenges

Why you should read the book

- It provides a useable framework to address employee motivation problems
- It provides easy to use tools and guides
- It provides specific examples of how to use the framework, tools, and guides

The author's qualifications to write the book

- Widely educated and has broadly studied the subject
- Years of consulting and coaching experience
- Tested and proven tools and guides

1

The Gap Between Theory and Application

Whenever I talk with a group of managers about performance, sooner or later, the talk always turns to the problem of motivating their employees. It has reached the point that I discourage anyone from using the word motivation in my workshops, coaching sessions, and consulting engagements. Too many managers want to use motivation as a black box to justify their own inability to improve performance. Get managers going on the subject and you will hear some variation on the theme "If I could only get good people...." Upon inquiry, what they mean by good people is people who will do what is needed without supervision. When it is pointed out that if, indeed, workers would perform successfully without supervision, then all management jobs would be redundant and could be eliminated—let's just say, it gives them something to think about.

More Than Theory Needed

Having spent the majority of my working life helping organizations improve productivity, I have read and heard more than a few theories about how to motivate employees to perform better. From theories such as Abraham Maslow's *Hierarchy of Needs* to advice in pop business books like Ken Blanchard's, *Who Moved My Cheese*, managers continue to struggle to come up with more effective ways to improve output. Most managers have been exposed to classic theories such as Frederick Hertzberg's *Satisfiers and Motivators* and Douglas McGregor's *Theory X and Theory* Y at some point in their work life. While they find these theories interesting, they also find that the theories come up short when trying to work with their employees in the real work world.

These managers have also been exposed to all sorts of psychobabble about feedback, reinforcement, self-esteem, and empowerment. They feel that these concepts don't help them much when faced with the real world challenge of motivating their people.

The Role of Improvement Initiatives

Companies have spent millions of dollars on improvement efforts such as work-study, quality circles, and re-engineering with varying degrees of success. Most of these initiatives, when they produced any improvement at all only worked for a portion of their employees and, even then, the improvements reached a plateau within months.

That's not to say that all the work and study on performance improvement has been wasted. That body of knowledge helped clarify the thinking about what motivates people in the workplace. Still most managers feel like the information is difficult, if not impossible, to apply in their daily work environment.

Practical Framework Needed

Most front line managers feel they need a framework that they can apply in their workplace. One manager, in utter frustration, blurted out "What I need to know is what to do to get Shirley to get her work in on time!" That statement summarized the crux of the problem with theories of motivation. They don't answer this type of question for that manager.

After fifteen years of working with organizations to help improve performance, the answer I have for that manager is frustrating and quite simple. Managers can't motivate those they manage to do anything. Motivation is an inside job. The motivation must come from Shirley.

When managing people to increase performance, motivation is not part of the equation.

That is a pretty dramatic statement, so let me phrase it another way to make certain that I am communicating clearly. As a manager, there is nothing you can do to motivate a worker to perform.

Can A Manager Motivate?

In his groundbreaking research for the book *Good to Great*, Jim Collins found that companies that make the transition from good performance to outstanding performance had certain elements in common. One key difference was that they didn't try to change people, but rather made certain that their people were doing the jobs where they performed well. Collins uses the analogy of the organization as a bus. The first step was to get the right people on the bus and to make sure those already on the bus are in the right seats. He points to the example of Nucor Steel. The company didn't try to motivate existing steelworkers to produce. Instead, they moved their plants to areas where the workforce had a strong work ethic and then taught them how to make steel.

The researched-based business book *First Break All The Rules* goes further with this thinking. It asserts people don't change and reinforces Collins point about getting the right people on the bus. While it has come under a great deal of discussion, former General Electric CEO Jack Welch's approach of cutting the low performing ten percent of your workforce each year certainly supports and grows out of this idea that an organization should get the right people.

Role of Incentives

You might be thinking to yourself "What about incentive compensation?" If you provide a financial incentive to do something, doesn't that motivate the individual? Don't programs such as stock options, bonuses, and pay for performance motivate employees? No! Incentive systems merely link pay to performance. These systems may help companies control overhead by not paying people who don't produce. That isn't the same thing as motivating an individual to do something in the first place. Look at entry level commissioned sales positions if you think incentives are effective in motivation. Here is an environment that is a pure incentive-based system—if you don't sell, you don't earn! If incentives were the magic to motivation, all of the people hired into those commissioned-based environments would be successful and highly motivated. The reality, of course, is that most entry level commissioned sales positions are ones that experience high turnover and even higher rates of marginal success. So, while many companies continue their commitment to incentive systems, these systems aren't really motivationally based.

Role of Positive Feedback

What about positive feedback, you might ask? Most current management thinking deals with the value of providing positive feedback to motivate future performance. Of course, by its very nature, feedback also comes after the performance. While it may have a role in forming behavior over time, feedback won't get people to establish a new behavior. The term Behavioral Psychologist B.F. Skinner used was operant conditioning. That is a fairly accurate description about how feedback works to reinforce behavioral trends. So, operant conditioning in the form of post performance feedback might be used to form a worker's behavior or to teach a mouse how to run a maze. But would you say the mouse was motivated to run the maze?

Motivation Is Different

Motivation is something entirely different. If this kind of behavioral modification isn't motivation, and if incentive compensation and positive feedback isn't motivation, then what is it? Let's turn to that question next.

Summary: The Gap Between Theory and Application

Managers are frustrated by theory that doesn't tell them what to do to solve real workplace motivation problems

Improvement initiatives only work for a portion of the organization and often have only a short-term impact

Managers have only a limited ability to impact employee motivation

Incentive systems don't produce lasting motivation

2

What is Motivation?

While many managers throw the term motivation around, few have given thought to what it really means. The root of the word is motive. Motive comes from the Latin word *motivus*, meaning moving; or *motivum*, meaning moving cause. The *Webster's Unabridged Dictionary* defines motive as "some inner drive, impulse, or intention that causes a person to do something or act." The same resource goes on to talk about motivating as "to furnish with a motive, incite, or to give impetus."

An Inner Drive That Creates Movement

The underlying focus of all these definitions is the feeling of movement. Movement is external. A person's movement is outward behavior. It can be observed. If it can be observed, it can be measured. Ironically, however, motives are, by their very nature and by definition, inner drives. As such, they can't be seen, or measured, or even known to be present. We can only observe the outward behavior and guess what motivates any action. Many times, in fact, people are not clear about their own motivation to act. Therapists generate millions of dollars in fees each year trying to help people answer the simple question "Why did I do that?" So we will define motivation in terms of the inner drives that activate and energize a person to act. Our working definition is:

Motivation is an internal directional force that activates and energizes a person to do something or act in a certain way.

Management of Motivation

As managers, we cannot manage inner drives. We can observe, measure, and manage behaviors. So, by definition, we cannot manage motivation, only behavior. Motivation is an inner state. As such it is unapproachable and mysterious to an outsider. Behavior is outward activity and can be managed. This is a very difficult concept for many managers to accept and incorporate into their management style. We will consider two case studies to clarify what management can do to influence an employee's motivation.

Case Study: There's Something About Mary

Fred is a front line supervisor for a large service firm. While working with his firm, Fred shared with me that he was very concerned about one of his workers, Mary. When I asked him what seemed to be the problem with Mary, he replied that she wasn't very highly motivated. I asked Fred what made him feel that Mary wasn't motivated. He replied that she didn't look motivated. "What about her looks make you feel that she isn't motivated, Fred?" I asked as a follow up. After several more probes from me, Fred finally focused in on Mary's posture (stoop shouldered), how she walked (she shuffled slowly), and her facial expression (she always looked sad).

At this point, I started questioning Fred about Mary's productivity compared to other workers. It seemed that Mary was a bit slower than most of the crew, but other than that her work was satisfactory. At this point I got Fred to focus on Mary's speed and had him coach her on techniques that would help her speed up. Within a week, Mary was producing as much as most of the others on the crew. Fred was still not happy, however, with her motivation.

When questioned, Fred focused once again on her demeanor. "She never smiles", he pointed out. "I don't think she's very happy to be here," he said. When I asked him why that was important, he had difficulty answering. He finally focused on his belief that happy workers are more productive.

Fred's Cultural Trance

This type of statement is what I like to refer to as a cultural trance. A cultural trance is something that most people in a particular environment believe to be true. For years, most people thought the world was flat. That, of course, didn't make the world flat. It did, however, keep many sailors from venturing out towards the horizon.

Fred's cultural trance (that happy workers are more productive) is at the root of a great deal of wasted management time. Fred wanted to figure out what he could do to get Mary to smile all the time. My suggestion was that he simply ask Mary to smile. He replied, "But that would be forced. She wouldn't really be happy here. She would just be acting."

Fred wanted to get inside Mary's head and motivate her to be happy with her work. He wanted her to show her motivation (the inward state) by a smiling face (the outward behavior). Many managers fall into the same trap. They focus on an employee's motivation rather than the behavior.

The reality is that if Mary produces at or above average she is a good employee and a manager can do nothing to influence her inner state. That manager can, however, make their behavioral expectations clear to Mary and provide feedback to her that will let her know how she is doing compared to what they expected. However, this molding of behavior is not motivation. Remember that motivation is an inner drive. However, the job of a manager is not to produce an inner state in a group of workers. It is to manage that group of workers so they get the work done.

Case Study: Teaching Lawyers to Sell

Of course, there are many other approaches that managers use to motivate workers. Susan, the managing partner of a small regional law firm wanted to motivate the firm's associates to market their services to potential clients. She had made that expectation very clear to each associate. Susan had even hired an outside consultant to train them in practice building (that's what lawyers call selling) skills.

Sitting beside me at a business lunch, Susan and I exchanged pleasantries until she found out what I did. Then she started telling me some of the difficulty her firm had encountered in trying to change the associates' behavior so that they would bring in new business. She wanted to know what else the firm could do. She had even considered the idea of weeding out the new associates that weren't successful with their marketing attempts. I asked her how many were successful and she said that very few had achieved success. "Why aren't they motivated," she asked? Susan was extremely disappointed when I responded with "I don't know, why don't we just ask them that question?"

I agreed to attend a meeting with a group of the associates to facilitate a discussion around the issue of marketing and motivation. After about twenty minutes of discussion, one of the associates blurted out "I don't market because I am afraid." Further probing yielded more information such as:

- "I'm afraid I don't know what I am doing."
- "I am afraid that I'll come off as looking dumb."
- "I don't want to seem like a salesman to our potential clients."

The fears rolled out like a great wave. You see, lawyers are competent and forceful in the law. But, when Susan moved them out of that environment, they felt awkward and unsure of themselves. These were feelings those young lawyers were not quite used to or ready to accept and process.

The fact was, those lawyers were motivated. Unfortunately for Susan, they were motivated not to sell! The result was that they found creative and plausible reasons to not market. In other words, their motivation that moved them away from marketing was stronger than their motivation towards marketing. So to motivate them to market, Susan had to find some way to help them manage and direct this motivation not to market. The benefits of marketing were external and long-term. The fear was internal and immediate. The fear won.

Susan, the managing partner, was confusing *Can Do* factors with *Will Do* factors.

Can Do Factors

Can Do factors have nothing to do with motivation. *Can Do* factors concern the skills a worker needs to do the work. *Can Do* factors can be trained. If I am working with salespeople, I can train them to repeat the features and benefits of each item in the product line. If I am working with accountants, I can train them in *Generally Accepted Accounting Principles*. These are skills they need to do the job. However, just because they know these skills doesn't mean they will do the job. Just because the lawyers are taught marketing skills, doesn't mean they're going to go out and market.

Managers constantly focus on *Can Do* factors when trying to address performance problems. The first step for many organizations in dealing with a performance problem is to send the under-performing employee to training.

This seldom works and is usually a complete waste of time and money. That's because the problem is seldom a *Can Do* problem. If an employee that has completed the basic training for a job is not performing, it is seldom a *Can Do* problem. It is usually a *Will Do* problem.

Will Do Factors

I worked with a company that spent great sums of money training their sales people, most of whom were not successful and soon left the company. Our firm was hired to address the turnover problem. After a few post-separation interviews, the problem quickly became clear. The people were leaving because they couldn't stand the constant rejection that came with the entry-level sales position. They left because their egos were so deflated they couldn't stand coming to work any more. The Director of Human Resources wanted to design a program to teach emotional resilience skills. She wanted to teach the people how to cope with and emotionally recover from the constant rejection they faced in the job. She was surprised by my reaction which was "Don't waste your money."

Emotional resilience is not something to train in a business environment. That's something that people go into intensive therapy to address. Our suggestion was to build a simulation into the interview process to help the company identify people that already had emotional resilience.

Will Do factors deal directly with motivation. *Will Do* factors determine what a person will try to do and what a person will keep doing. *Will Do* factors fall into the realm of motivation.

Summary: What is Motivation

Motivation is an internal directional force that activates and energizes a person to do something or act in a certain way.

Happy workers aren't necessarily more productive.

Just because an employee can perform a task (*Can Do*), doesn't mean they will perform that task (*Will Do*).

Will Do factors fall into the realm of motivation.

3

Two Motivators Managers Need to Know

If you haven't studied classic motivation theory, this chapter will be easier for you to accept. If you have been through training on classic motivation theory, forget Maslow's *Hierarchy of Needs*. Throw Hertzberg's *Satisfiers* in the trash. Cook up *Theory X and Theory Y* in alphabet soup! There are only two motivators.

We touched on the first great motivator when relating the experience with the law firm associates. What was the internal drive that motivated them to not market? It was fear. Fear is the first great motivator.

Fear Motivation

Fear is a powerful motivator. The stronger the fear, the stronger the motivation. We have all heard stories about ordinary people who performed courageous acts under stress. Many, when interviewed, explain that they really didn't think about what they did. They just did it. If they had thought about it, they may have not done it.

Limitations of Fear as a Motivator

It's Unpredictable

Fear motivates directly and viscerally, often bypassing the logic circuits that usually moderate our willingness to take risks. Ironically, however, fear also paralyzes. Some people, faced with the same set of circumstances, do nothing. So the unpredictable nature of fear makes it unreliable as a motivator because you can't really predict if it will get someone moving or paralyze him or her to the point of inaction.

It's Scarcity Based

Managers have known about the motivational power of fear for a very long time. Many have used it to their advantage by threatening to withhold some benefit or impose some unwanted sanction to manipulate a worker into performing. This creates an atmosphere of scarcity that taps into a worker's internal motivation through fear. The more scarcity in a society, the better fear works as a motivator. As our society becomes increasingly affluent, fear becomes a less powerful motivator. If jobs are plentiful, a manager can't trigger the fear of being fired because the worker can simply go and get another job. Even if I am at the bottom of the economic ladder, fear doesn't work well. If, for instance, I am an entry-level service worker, I have many options of where to work. If the McDonald's manager tries to use fear to motivate me, I just walk next door and work for Burger King.

It's Source Dependent

For fear to be effective, the source of the fear must be present. If I work because I am afraid of the boss, when the boss isn't present, I slow down. The source of the fear must be constantly present to trigger the employee's internal motivation.

It's Subject to Habituation

Habituation is a biological fact. Our bodies respond to differences in the environment. If a stimulus is constantly present, we tend not to notice it. Ironically enough, the fear stimulus must be present to motivate, but if it is constantly present, we get habituated to it and do not respond as readily. So the motivational power of fear diminishes over time. To avoid this habituation effect, some manager's resort to an ever-escalating level of fear.

When Will Fear Motivate

Remember that the root of motivation has to do with movement. Fear is a valuable motivator when it is used to start or stop a behavior.

Ego Motivation

The second great motivator is ego. Ego is the internal force of attraction that pulls an individual toward a thing, an idea, a location, or a person. Ego is also a powerful motivator, causing people to overcome astounding obstacles, endure great hardships, and expend superhuman effort to attain the object or state that attracts them.

Limitations of Ego as a Motivator

It's Difficult to Channel

Ego is, by nature, very individualistic. As such, it may be challenging to channel an ego motivation into a particular direction or funnel it into a particular cause. So, unless the ego motivation takes the individual in the same direction as the organization, it may be hard for a manager to direct that force into the organization's direction.

It's Difficult to Moderate

Ego is, no doubt, the force that motivated Harlen Sanders to create the Kentucky Fried Chicken Empire in his late sixties. It's also the same force that drove an unemployed artist named Adolph Hitler to rise and take control of Germany in the 1930's. Ego motivation is often difficult to moderate. Every organization has at least one prima donna highly productive individual that is also a nightmare to manage.

It's Individualistic

You can't institutionalize ego motivation into incentive systems, evaluation forms, and feedback loops. Ego motivation is so individualistic that it varies dramatically from person to person.

It's Addictive

Like a drug addict, the individual that tastes the rush of ego motivation can become addicted to the feeling of power. It can lead them to exercise poor judgment, become difficult to work with, and trigger roller coaster ups and downs in their performance.

When Will Ego Motivate?

Ego is a versatile motivator that works in a wide variety of situations. In fact, the only time ego doesn't work is when there is a fear motivator present that is stronger than the ego motivator.

Two Determinants to Motivation

For this information to be practically useful to a manager, they must have a framework to help them diagnose what internal motivation is stimulating an external behavior. They also need some guidelines on how to respond in a way that may stimulate an individual to choose to move from one motivational source to another.

There are two determinants for motivation. The first is Locus of Control.

Locus of Control

Locus of Control is a concept used to describe how much control an individual feels they have over a given situation or action. It is a continuum with External

Fig. 3.1

Control at one end, where the individual feels they have absolutely no control over the situation. At the other end is Internal Control, where the individual feels they have absolute control over the situation. This can be represented as illustrated in **Fig. 3.1**.

Perceived Value

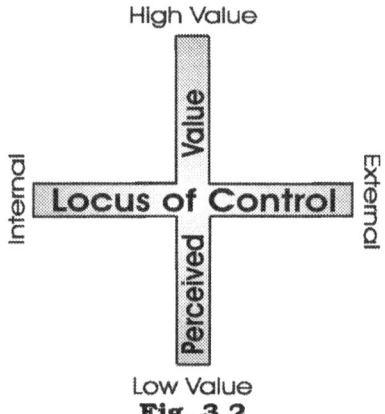

High Value

Low Value

Fig. 3.2

The second determinant for motivation is Perceived Value. Perceived Value is the value that an individual holds for a particular thing or the outcome to a set of circumstances. So the determinants of Locus of Control and Perceived Value create a grid illustrated in **Fig. 3.2**.

If a thing or set of circumstances has a high Perceived Value and an external Locus of Control (I have no control), we label our response to that set of circumstances *Fear*.

If a thing or set of circumstances has high Perceived Value and an internal Locus of Control, we can refer to it as *Ego*. If the thing has low Perceived Value and an external Locus of Control, we'll call our response Apathy. If a thing has low Perceived Value and an internal Locus of Control, our response to it is Assumed. So, including the labels for the four quadrants, the grid is illustrated in **Fig. 3.3**.

This grid is called the Motivational Vector Grid. You'll learn more about how to use this tool in the next chapter.

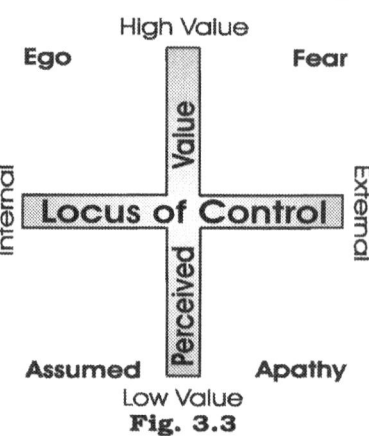

High Value

Ego   Fear

Assumed   Apathy

Low Value

Fig. 3.3

Summary: Two Motivators Managers Need to Know

There are two great motivators: Fear and Ego

- Fear is effective when used to start or stop a behavior
- Ego works in a variety of circumstances. A stronger Fear motivator can stifle it.

Limitations of Fear as a motivator

- It's unpredictable
- It's scarcity based
- It's source dependent
- It's subject to habituation

Limitations of Ego as a motivator

- It's difficult to channel
- It's difficult to moderate
- It's individualistic
- It's addictive

There are two determinants that stimulate motivation

- Locus of Control
- Perceived Value

4

Managing Determinants and the Laws of Motivational Vectors

I said earlier that a manager really couldn't motivate an employee to do anything. Since motivation is defined as an internal force, there is no way that a manager (being external) can directly access, observe, or manipulate that internal force in the employee. Hence, there is no direct way for managers to motivate the employee. That's the bad news.

The good news is that a manager can manipulate the environment so as to have an impact on Locus of Control and Perceived Value. The manager, by influencing the environment, can have an indirect influence on the employee's motivation.

An employee can get stuck in a cycle of non-performance in any one of the four quadrants. The key to changing performance is moving the employee along the continuum of either Locus of Control or Perceived Value to jump-start the employee's own motivation to perform. Using this framework, the manager's job in motivation becomes to determine where the employee's response falls on this grid. Once established, the manager can manipulate the environment by changing variables that influence either the Locus of Control or the Perceived Value. That change in the environment causes the employee to move into another area of the grid.

Let's return to the problem with turnover of new salespeople mentioned earlier for a specific example of how to use the grid.

Case Study: You Don't Know Jack

Consider the case of Jack, a new hire to the sales force. Jack completed his basic sales training and came to the office the beginning of his first day with his motivation firmly in the Ego quadrant as illustrated in **Fig. 4.1.** Jack learned all the features and benefits of his offering in sales training. He had practiced a planned presentation to the point where he could deliver it with finesse and ease. He had carefully studied the company's proven techniques for uncovering and overcoming objections. Most importantly, he had learned all the killer closes

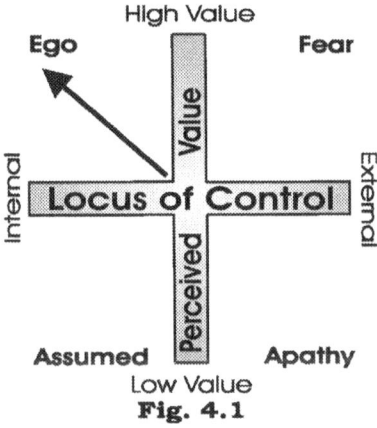

Fig. 4.1

that had worked so reliably for the company's other sales people over the years. Jack set down at his desk, opened the portfolio of leads his manager had supplied and began making phone calls.

Unfortunately for Jack, the prospects he was calling hadn't attended the same wonderful sales training as Jack. They didn't know their lines as well as Jack knew his own. By lunchtime Jack had moved from an internal Locus of Control to an external Locus of Control. He no longer felt that he had all the answers or even knew what to expect each time he picked up the phone to dial. Jack had moved from Ego to Fear on the grid as illustrated in **Fig 4.2.**

The situation only continued to deteriorate. By the end of the second week, Jack was going to lunch with the other new sales people where they all discussed how poorly all the techniques they learned in sales training worked on real-world prospective customers. In fact, they were starting to question if they would ever earn the kind of commissions they had been assured during the hiring process were possible. In other words, they were moving from high Perceived Value (If I do this, I will earn a high commission) to low Perceived Value (It is not possible to earn the kind of money I

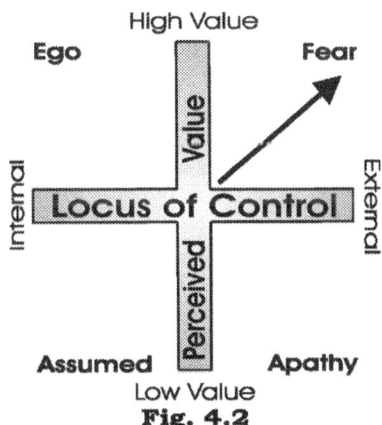

Fig. 4.2

thought I could earn here). In other words, they were all moving from Fear to Apathy on the grid as illustrated in **Fig 4.3**.

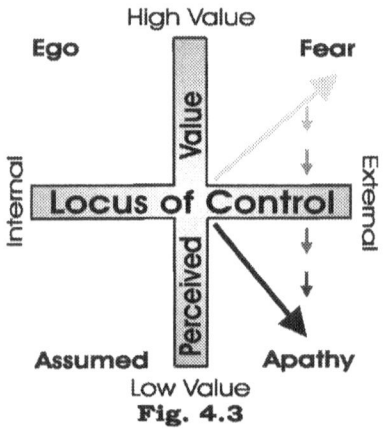

Fig. 4.3

Is it any wonder that this company experienced high turnover in this sales force?

To alleviate this problem, the company needed to develop an approach that would keep the new salespeople in the Ego quadrant. As things stood, the new salespeople came to work thinking their jobs were to close sales. In other words, their job was to get people to make a decision to spend money for their company's service. They were all on commission, so the Perceived Value was all tied to closing sales. Unfortunately, the company's offering was a high-dollar value conceptual sale. Of all the prospects the company identified and qualified, only about ten percent of them actually wound up making a purchase. The company, thinking that this low closing percentage might discourage the new sales people, chose not to share that average with them. As a result, most of the new sales staff came to the position with an unrealistically high expectation of what percentage of the prospects would actually buy.

So the first change the company made was to re-frame this entry-level sales position from sales person to prospect qualifier. As a sales person, all the Perceived Value was attached to closing sales. As a prospect qualifier, there was a spectrum of outcomes that all held Perceived Value. It was important to discover the prospects' financial condition, their timeframes, and their decision making process. This shift in emphasis allowed the company to keep the front-line staff in the ego quadrant for a long time because the staff was able to experience the payoff for the Perceived Value on a regular basis. The company went on to re-engineer their sales process to create a two-tiered system where the junior level people qualified and a more experienced person actually closed the sale. This change reduced turnover, lowered overall costs, and improved sales.

Let's take another example.

Case Study: Getting Doug To Sell

TechSys provided on-site technical services to a large business oriented client base. The company was diversifying and expanding its range of service offerings to try to increase its revenue and account penetration. As part of this initiative, the company had trained all of the service representatives in the new service offerings, mentored them on some basic sales skills, and created an incentive compensation system. All of these changes were designed to motivate the service representatives to sell the customer some of the new services while they were interacting with the customers on service calls.

Doug, a reliable and responsive technical service representative, drew the attention of his manager. After six months, he had failed to make one sale for the new services. In talking with Doug, John, the manager, uncovered several pieces of information:

1. Doug thought of sales people as sleazy, slick talkers and he didn't think of himself as a sales type. In other words, Doug was motivated away from selling the new services because he didn't want to think of himself in the same category as a salesperson. This ego motivator was the force motivating Doug. His sense of self was something he had control over and it had high Perceived Value. Unfortunately, these forces were motivating him away from selling the new services.

2. Doug believed that his job was really to provide technical service to his customers. He also felt that, if the customers wanted to buy the new services, they would ask him about them. Doug felt that the company's sales people would take care of promoting the new services. In other words, Doug assumed that he had the power to define his job. In addition, he felt that selling the new services was someone else's job. He thought selling was something in the sales people's control and that selling had limited Perceived Value to him.

3. Doug felt that, because of his superior technical ability in providing the current types of customer service, his job was very secure, whether he sold the new services or not. That is to say that Doug thought the company's assessment of his competence was totally in his control and that the possibility that he would be held accountable for selling had limited Perceived Value because his technical skills would see him through.

In Doug's case there is a compound motivation system. There are multiple motivational forces at work. These motivational forces are called Motivational Vectors. The addition of Motivational Vectors to the Grid creates a tool that allows a manager to begin applying this framework in the real world.

Using Motivational Vectors

In mathematics, vectors have properties of both magnitude and direction. The same is true with Motivational Vectors.

In Doug's case, the first motivational determinant that surfaced was the ego force of his self-image and view about salespeople. Mapping that on a Motivational Vector Grid, it might look like **Fig 4.4**.

The line, labeled *Self-Image*, represents Doug's motivation. It shows both the strength (by the length) and direction of his motivation. You can clearly see that Doug is in the Ego Quadrant with this Motivational Vector.

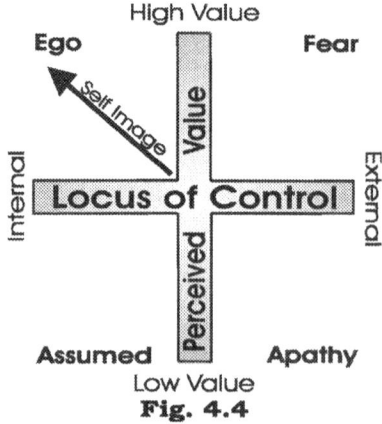

Fig. 4.4

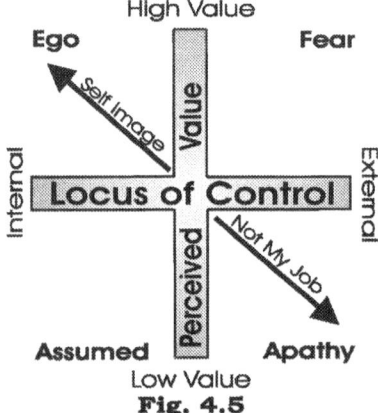

Fig. 4.5

There is a second Motivational Vector operating here as well. Remember that Doug believed (in spite of what his manager said) that selling was someone else's job (an external Locus of Control) and, thus, had limited Perceived Value to him. That creates a Motivational Vector, labeled *Not My Job*, in the Apathy quadrant, shown in **Fig. 4.5**.

There is also a third Motivational Vector in play in this situation. Remember that Doug believed he had the control to define his job responsibilities (again, in spite of what his manager said). He also felt that his strong technical abilities (which are completely within his internal Locus of Control) would override his manager's guidance to perform the new role. In other words he ignored the possibility that his manager might fire him if he didn't perform the required selling tasks. This creates a Motivational Vector, labeled *Not Fired*, in the Assumed quadrant as illustrated in **Fig 4.6**.

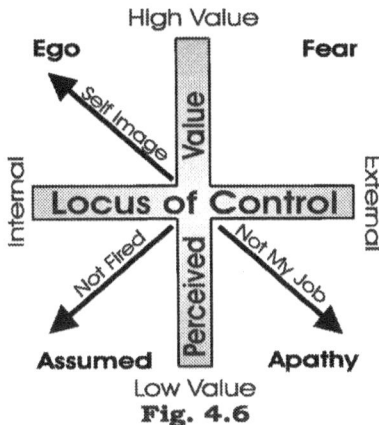

Fig. 4.6

First Law of Motivational Vectors

Just like with the laws of physics, there are predictable relationships in Motivational Vectors. The first law of Motivational Vectors is: *without outside intervention, the sum of the Motivational Vectors in any situation produces a stasis that will not change.* In other words, unless you do something to stimulate action, an employee will stay stuck just where they are!

Second Law of Motivational Vectors

That brings us to the second law of Motivational Vectors. *In order to break stasis, an outside intervention must exert a force strong enough to cause some significant change in direction or strength of an existing Motivational Vector.* The stronger the existing Motivational Vector, the stronger the intervention needed to have an impact.

Looking at Doug's Motivational Vector Grid, the Motivational Vector that represents his ego motivation arising from his self-image and view of salespeople is strong. To change that, an equally strong (or stronger) intervention will be needed. If Doug's manager hasn't analyzed this, a typical managerial response might be to try to impose some form of "do this, or else." However, because of the limits of organizational power, this fear vector is usually not strong enough to counteract Doug's ego vector. In too many cases, the managerial response to that ineffectiveness is for the manager to label Doug a problem employee with an attitude.

This labeling, of course, serves to allow the manager to absolve him or her self from all responsibility in this situation. In this example, it discounts John's inability to act, blaming the problem on Doug instead. It allows John to feel okay about writing Doug off and doing nothing further to create an environment where Doug chooses to perform successfully (to be motivated).

Third Law of Motivational Vectors

That brings us to the third law of Motivational Vectors: *when they're stuck, it's always your move.*

In other words, it is the very foundation of managerial work to create an environment where the employee chooses to perform successfully. If the employee is stuck in some unsuccessful pattern of non-performance, it is the manager's job to do something! If a manager says, "I've done all I can; there's nothing more I can do." That isn't a condemnation of the employee; it is a reflection on the manager's skill. The manager's job is to always have another option to try.

Fourth Law of Motivational Vectors

That leads to the fourth law of Motivational Vectors. *If what you are doing now isn't working, anything else is better.*

For every problem employee there is a problem manager. A problem manager is a manager who has stopped trying. Of course, that also signals that there is an organizational dysfunction because it means that there is someone above that manager who has also either given up or, even worse, is not aware of the situation and allows it to continue from ignorance or apathy.

Some readers, at this point, may be saying to themselves, "Now wait a minute; there are some people you just can't do anything with. They're impossible!" I agree. There are some people a manager can't do anything with. But that isn't a statement about the employee, it is an admission of inadequacy or a lack of development on the manager's part.

Unfortunately, most organizations don't make it acceptable or safe for a manager to admit that they need help in developing additional strategies and tactics to try with someone like Doug. It is acceptable to label and discount Doug, however, as an attitude problem.

So how would a manager use the Motivational Vector Grid to create an environment where Doug will choose to do the sales work?

The purpose of the Motivational Vector Grid is to help a manager diagnose the motivational forces that are influencing a particular employee's behavior and to analyze options for intervention. We just gave an example of analyzing the motivational forces that were influencing Doug's behavior. Now, let's go on to analyze the options available to Doug's manager in making an intervention.

Consider the ego vector for Doug. Here Doug's self-image about himself and his internal picture of salesmen are pulling him away from the desired behavior. One option is for Doug's manager to use a fear vector. Assuming of course, that the manager has the authority to threaten Doug's job, the manager could use Doug's fear of losing his job to exert a motivational force larger than the ego vector. This may or may not stimulate Doug to perform the desired task. This intervention might also motivate him to look for another job!

Fifth Law of Motivational Vectors

There is a fifth law of Motivational Vectors. *The further away from the current Motivational Vector, the more motivational power is needed to create movement.* You can see from the direction and force of Doug's ego vector that it would take a large fear vector to create enough momentum to cause Doug to change direction. If, however, John chooses a motivational force closer to the existing vector, it will take less effort to cause a change in direction. So, it would be easier for John to use a Motivational Vector in the same quadrant as Doug's current motivation—that is, an ego motivator. John should try to find something that is high in importance and that Doug feels is within his control.

For instance, John could appeal to Doug's sense of himself as a creative and resourceful individual, challenging him to come up with an approach to selling that was not sleazy. The conversation might go something like this:

Doug, I know how you feel about sales people. They seem like a sleazy bunch of low lifes to you. That kind of perception might be one of the reasons the company has asked the technical staff to become involved in the sales process. I've seen the creativity and resourcefulness you've demonstrated in solving our customer's technical problems. That's why I have a great deal of confidence that you can apply that same creative ability to the challenge of selling these new services to our customers. You're better than those sleazy salespeople are and I know you can do this in a professional manner and maintain that strong sense of integrity that makes you such a valuable member of the technical team. Is this something you would like to work on alone, or would you rather put a team together to attack this challenge?

Notice how many times John has appealed to Doug's ego; how he dangles bait trying to hook it to stimulate that internal motivation.

Looking at the second Motivational Vector for Doug, we see that he is apathetic about selling because he thinks it is someone else's job. Now, the manager could try to find something that was high in importance and within Doug's Locus of Control (an ego motivator) to cause Doug to change his motivation on this item. However, an ego motivator would have to be of sufficient strength to turn the apathy vector 180 degrees. Notice that the manager could move Doug off the apathy vector with a fear motivator with much less effort.

That conversation might go something like this:

Doug, I have noticed that you haven't sold any of the new services yet. Perhaps I wasn't clear with you how important that part of your job is. There are two things you might want to consider. First, your record on selling the new services will make up 25% of your evaluation coming up in three months. If you stay where you are, that will bring your overall evaluation down from last year's above average to a marginal rating. From my interaction with you, I feel sure you don't want that to happen.

Second, as you know, the company is under competitive pressures like never before. While there is nothing definite, it is a real possibility that the technical staff may need to be downsized next year. When the decision is made as to who goes and who stays, you can be sure that performance in selling these new services will be a major factor. I wouldn't want to see you in the at risk group. Is there something more that I can do to help you get started?

This conversation may be enough to stimulate Doug to action. Notice that John also ends the conversation with an offer to help. Before we move on to a more in-depth look at how to artfully manage the environment to stimulate change in Motivational Vectors, lets review the five laws.

Summary: Five Laws of Motivational Vectors

1. Without outside intervention, the sum of the Motivational Vectors in any situation produces a stasis that will not change.

2. In order to break stasis; an outside intervention must exert a force large enough to cause some significant change in direction or strength of an existing Motivational Vector.

3. When they're stuck, it's always your move.

4. If what you are doing now isn't working, anything else is better.

5. The further away from the current Motivational Vector, the more motivational power is needed to create movement.

5

Managing Perceived Value

So, we have set forth the proposition that a manager cannot manage motivation, but rather only manage the environment to impact an individual's motivation. More specifically, we have targeted two elements of the environment that impact motivation and may be influenced by management actions: Perceived Value and Locus of Control.

If you do not accept this proposition, or at least are not willing to explore the implications for managers if it is true, then you may as well shut this book and invest your time elsewhere.

If you get to this paragraph, then I will assume that you are, at a minimum, willing to explore the potential implications if what we have said so far is accurate.

Let's start by examining the areas that deal with Perceived Value where a manager can have some positive influence.

There are four factors that impact Perceived Value that a manager can influence:

1. Focus of the Pay Value

2. Size of the Pay Value

3. Immediacy of the Pay Value

4. Attainability of the Pay Value

Focus of the Pay Value

Many managers, when thinking of the Pay Value that goes with work, quickly become too narrowly focused on economic Pay Value. While there can be no doubt that economic Pay Value can be an important factor in motivation, it tends to get undeserved attention from management and human resource people. The five factors that a manager can use to influence Perceived Value are summarized in **Fig. 5.1** and explained in detail in the rest of this chapter.

Economic Pay Value

Economic Pay Value consists of the money, benefits, and other substitutes for monetary reward, such as stock options. Typically when a manager makes economic Pay Value the primary focus it can back fire on him or her.

Focus of Pay Value

Economic
Money
Benefits
Stock Options/Ownership

Self Efficacy
Successful Performance
Vicarious Performance
Persuasive Feedback
Mental Rehearsal

Psychological Integration
Living congruent with my vision

Social Integration
Belonging
Affiliating with others

Power and Control

Fig 5.1

Case Study—Martisha Earns a Raise

Let's look at the case of Martisha. Martisha is a front line service worker in Baltimore, Maryland. She is single, graduated from college four years ago, and works at a Help Desk Support position for a large professional firm. She has a pile of college debt, no car (because she cannot afford it), and lives in a one-bedroom apartment in an edgy section just north of the downtown business core. She makes $28,000 a year. Albert, Martisha's manager, rated her outstanding in her recently completed performance evaluation and gave her a $1,000 raise.

I first learned about Martisha while coaching Albert. He was surprised by Martisha's reaction to her raise. She not only didn't seem to appreciate the fact that he had gone out on a limb to get her that raise, but actually seemed to be resentful. It seemed like she was actually almost insulted by it.

Let's look at it from Martisha's standpoint for a moment. She is paid 26 times a year. So, that $1,000 amounts to a gross increase of just about $38.50 a pay period. That's about $3.60 a workday. After taxes and FICA, of course, it's substantially less than that. So, for busting her hump all year, she doesn't even get enough to have lunch at McDonalds each day! It gets worse, because as Martisha talks with her co-workers, she finds out that her friend, an average performer at work, got a $500 raise. That means all the extra effort she put in to earn her outstanding performance only earned her $1.80 per day more than the average performer. So that effort only earned her enough to go to McDonalds every other day! I can't imagine why Martisha would be resentful of that after a year of hard work, can you?

The reality is that the economic Pay Value had almost no significant impact on the way Martisha lived. It didn't substantially improve her day to day life. That is true with most of the economic Pay Value offered by organizations to motivate their employees. It is too small to have a substantial positive impact on the way the employee lives. The incremental difference between an average performance and an outstanding performance (if this difference is recognized at all) is truly marginal compared to the extra effort required to earn that outstanding rating.

Of course, as I analyzed this situation with Albert, he pointed out that he wanted to give Martisha a larger raise, but his senior manager wouldn't allow it. The company simply couldn't afford it in the current uncertain economic times.

In the course of our discussion, it became clear that there was a benefit to Albert when his focus was on economic Pay Value. Albert, like most managers, has an external Locus of Control for economic Pay Value. In other words, they don't have the authority to dole out raises or increases in benefits. So, it is the company's fault that Martisha has an attitude problem now. So, by focusing on economic Pay Value with employees they distance themselves from the responsibility to engage the employee in a meaningful way.

The ironic thing about Martisha's situation is that the same senior manager that explained to Albert why he couldn't give Martisha a larger raise received a six-figure bonus at the end of the year, but that's a topic for another book.

Self-Efficacy

Self-Efficacy refers to the degree to which one feels they can do a particular task. It is the sense that one is capable to perform.

As I explored Martisha's reaction to her raise with Albert, one fact he had missed is that, despite her resentment about the size of the raise, she continued to perform in an outstanding manner. In his emotional reaction to Martisha's resentment, Albert had missed a Pay Value focus for her. Martisha was obviously focused on the sense of Self-Efficacy that she had from performing her job well. Management thinking has danced around this concept for years. Terms such as work ethic, attitude, pride in a job well done are all management code words for a strong sense of self-efficacy. Martisha had it in spite of the way she was managed.

Unfortunately her experience is not uncommon for above average performers in organizations. In most cases, they are above average performers because they have a strong sense of self-efficacy rather than because they are managed well or receive economic rewards commensurate with their effort.

It is important for a manager to recognize how workers form feelings of self-efficacy. There are four principal areas for influence: successful performance, vicarious experience, persuasive feedback, and mental rehearsal.

1. Successful Performance

If an employee successfully performs a task, generally speaking he or she will have a higher feeling of self-efficacy when performing that task in the future. Thus, it is important for a manager to take the time to increase the possibility of success before a worker tries to complete the task on his or her own. The military recognized this years ago when they developed their protocol for on-the-job training for new recruits. This approach demonstrates and explains the task so the individual can see it performed successfully. It also includes repetition where the learner explains the steps while the trainer performs them. All of these steps build self-efficacy before the new recruit attempts the task.

2. Vicarious Experience

Another frequently used technique to build feelings of self-efficacy is the use of vicarious experience. With this approach, an individual would observe another person successfully performing the task. The individual may also study such details as how that experienced person mentally prepares to perform the task. This approach works best if the person being observed is like the person that is observing. The person learning the new task should be able to relate to the experienced person to the point where they say to themselves, "if they can do it, surely I can do it."

3. Persuasive Feedback

This is usually labeled positive feedback or cheerleading. Most managers don't take full advantage of this tool to stimulate feelings of self-efficacy. They look at it as a superfluous reward that they shouldn't have to give someone to do a job they're already being paid to do. When a manager doesn't take the opportunity to provide this feedback, they miss the chance to enhance Pay Value by boosting the employee's feelings of self-efficacy.

4. Mental Rehearsal

Mental Rehearsal means having someone imagine successfully performing a task before they actually attempt it. Many managers dismiss mental rehearsal as some form of new-age mumbo-jumbo but there is a great deal of research that supports the reality that someone doesn't have to actually perform a task successfully to boost their sense of self-efficacy. Simply imagining the successful performance though mental rehearsal can also boost these feelings as well.

Psychological Integration

In addition to feeling a sense of self-efficacy, individuals may also have a Pay Value focus on making sense of their existence. Much writing about life stages highlights this focus of figuring out what's it all about for one's life. This need to figure out who we are and then live a life congruent with that vision is referred to as psychological integration.

To some extent, it was a crisis of psychological integration for Doug, our service representative from the previous chapter. He was having problems motivating himself to sell (or he was good at motivating himself not to sell) because selling activities didn't match up with the picture he held of himself. It wasn't like him to sell.

Social Integration

Social integration refers to a desire to create opportunities to interact and affiliate with others. The concept of belonging is a piece of it. But it is more than that. It's the motivational Pay Value focus that creates a drive to interact with family, friends, and neighbors. It's the focus that stimulates people to share part of their story with a complete stranger on an airplane. It's the focus that moves us to join civic, social, or business clubs. It's the focus that leads people to wear Harley Davidson tee shirts and Nike caps.

Walking down Walnut Street in Philadelphia with a client, we were approached by a panhandler who asked us for a quarter. I shook my head no, but my client reached in his pocket and gave the man a quarter. We walked on in silence for a few steps but soon my curiosity got the better of me. *"Why did you give him a quarter,"* I asked? *"Because my worst fear is that something will happen to me and I'll wind up like that,"* he quickly replied. *"I can imagine what it would feel like to be reduced to begging on the street and I hope if I approach someone they will be willing to help me."*

That client's motivational Pay Value focus was on social integration. He realized that somehow that panhandler and he were all part of the same human condition. He reached out because he accepted that fact.

Power and Control

Power and control refers to the degree to which one wants to influence people, events, and one's environment.

While interviewing Donald Trump about his success as a real estate developer in New York, a reporter asked him how much money was enough? At first, Trump looked puzzled by the question. Then he grinned and said, *"It's not about enough!"*

That response reveals another key focus for Pay Value for an individual—the feeling of power and control. The most obvious manifestations of this Pay Value focus come from the titans of industry and the heads of governments. It's what led a poor immigrant named Carnegie to build a monopoly in the steel business in the early 1900's and a well-to-do nerd named Gates to out maneuver a giant like IBM in the software business in the late 1900's. It is the same focus that led the son of a welfare mother named Clinton to push himself into the position of President of the United States.

However, it's not just titans of industry or top politicians that are moved by power and control.

Case Study: Andrea Tests Harriet's Patience

The case of Andrea is a perfect example. Andrea's boss Harriet frequently complained about her in coaching sessions. Harriet was frustrated because Andrea regularly came late to team meetings and sometimes missed them entirely. Andrea also missed project deadlines, usually only by a short time, often a matter of hours.

"*It seems like she is purposely testing my patience,*" Harriet explained. "*It seems like she is trying to get to me. Her work is excellent. She is very bright. She just seems to have an attitude problem towards authority.*"

She was so frustrated that she was starting to look for reasons to write up Andrea. Harriet was building a case to support firing her. In a last ditch effort to salvage Andrea, Harriet asked me to coach her.

At my fist meeting with Andrea, I asked her "*Why do you think Harriet wants you to participate in a coaching process?*" Andrea's response was very enlightening. She said, "*I suppose it's just another of her lame attempts to control me.*"

It turned out Andrea had a high sensitivity to power and control. She felt as if Harriet's management approach was all geared towards exerting power and showing off the control she had over employees. This instantly rubbed Andrea the wrong way. It led her to express her own power and control through tardiness, a very passive-aggressive outlet.

Size of the Pay Value

With an economic Pay Value focus, it is easy for most of us to understand that, if you make the size of the Pay Value larger it will increase an individual's motivation. It is surprising, therefor, that a manager can't generalize that to the other areas of Pay Value focus.

Managers who refuse to give positive feedback to boost a worker's sense of self-efficacy miss an opportunity to positively influence motivation. If you don't know much about a worker's values, goals, and lifestyle, there is little chance that you can successfully tap the power of psychological and/or social integration. If you bind workers up in rule-based management systems with multiple levels of approval needed for any action, it is highly unlikely that you can take full advantage of a power and control focus.

Case Study: Mary and the Professor

Mary is a good example of how large an impact one can have by increasing the size of the Pay Value. During a coaching session, I asked Mary to give me an example of someone in her life that had motivated her to high performance. Without hesitation, she told about a professor that she had 15 years earlier in college. As she explained:

He was the most demanding professor I had ever had! Most students hated him because he graded so hard. I got him for one of the required courses—you know the type where they don't tell you who is going to teach it and you get the luck of the draw. I was terrified when I showed up to the first class and it was him. In fact, he had such a reputation that I was thinking about dropping his class. Well, he may have been hard, but he was really good so I decided to tough it out. About the third week of class, he stopped me as I was leaving and asked, "What is your major?" I told him and then asked him why he wanted to know. He said, "because you can't hide talent, and you obviously have it." I was totally floored. Here was this brilliant man who had incredibly high standards telling me I had talent. It really got to me. I went on to become an honors student and wound up taking four more classes that he taught. The remark motivated me for the rest of my time in school.

Mary's professor had appealed to her sense of self-efficacy and psychological integration. It motivated her to higher performance for years. The size of the Pay Value is not always about money.

Immediacy of the Pay Value

One of the major limitations of all formal evaluation programs is that they institutionalize the idea that Pay Value is on some sort of artificially determined schedule. For most of the motivational focus areas we have discussed, the reality is that Pay Value can be delivered any time. The sooner an employee feels that they will receive a Pay Value, the more motivational force it will carry with it. With the exception of economic Pay Value, the manager has a great deal of latitude in determining the timing of the Pay Value. Most managers fail to take fullest advantage of Pay Value because they pay little or no attention to timing.

Attainability of the Pay Value

Attainability refers to the degree to which an individual feels they may realistically expect to receive a Pay Value.

Case Study: Marsha's Project

Marsha came into the peer group coaching meeting and she was obviously feeling down. When it came her turn to speak, she told the group what was troubling her:

I worked my butt off for the last three weeks finishing up that project for Danielle (her boss). It was a masterpiece! When I dropped it on her desk, she just grunted. It's been three days and I haven't heard a thing from her.

Marsha expected to get some positive feedback on her work, but didn't. This directly impacted her motivation by impacting multiple factors that influence her Perceived Value. Her sense of self-efficacy wavered. Her psychological and social integration suffered. Also, her feelings of power and control were diminished. As Marsha explained to the group:

Now I'm starting to wonder if the project was really any good at all. I thought it was when I turned it in, but since Danielle hasn't said anything, I'm starting to feel like she thinks my work is sub-standard (self-efficacy). *I thought Danielle had more respect for me than that* (Psychological Integration). *I thought she was my friend* (Social Integration). *I mean what do I have to do here to get my work recognized, anyway?* (Power and Control).

Obviously, Marsha was feeling that the Pay Value she was seeking was unattainable and it was de-motivating her performance.

So as a manager, focus on the factors impacting Pay Value that you can positively influence. This chapter has been an overview of those factors. In later chapters you will learn specific tools, techniques, and approaches to use.

Summary: Managing Perceived Value

Change the Focus of the Pay Value

1. Economic Pay Value

2. Self-efficacy

    Factors That Influence
    Successful Performance
    Vicarious Experience
    Persuasive Feedback
    Mental Rehearsal

3. Psychological Integration

4. Social Integration

5. Power and Control

Change the Size of the Pay Value

Change the Immediacy of the Pay Value

Change the Attainability of the Pay Value

6

Managing Locus of Control

Locus of Control means the degree to which an individual feels they have the power to act. When a worker feels like they have choices, that feeling directly impacts their perception of Locus of Control. Having a choice about something puts it in an individual's Locus of Control. In the context of the Motivational Grid, that gives us, as managers, a tool to influence where the worker's Motivational Vector will point. There are three variables a manager has the ability to influence: the number of choices a worker considers within their Locus of Control, the scope of the choices they feel is available to them, and the clarity of the choices.

Increasing the Number of Choices

There are a number of areas where a manager can increase the number of choices an employee makes, thereby influencing the worker's perception of Locus of Control. Generally speaking, management tends to over-control their employees—prescribing through policy, procedure, or custom, many day-to-day routines that could be turned back over to the employee to choose. They often control the details of the workday right down to something as basic as what time to show up.

Case Study: Ellen Takes Control

Ellen is a perfect case in point. Ellen's supervisor, Juan brought her to my attention as an attitude problem. *"She is constantly late for work,"* he explained.

In Juan's way of thinking, being late for work led to the forgone conclusion that one had an attitude problem. When I asked Juan why she was late for work, he said, "*I don't know, and I don't care. It's not my job to worry about her life outside of work. She is supposed to show up on time.*"

It turned out that on time meant 7:00 AM. She had to be there at 7:00 AM because that is the shift Juan had set for her in the schedule (taking a choice away from her). There was no policy or procedure that prescribed the shifts, merely convention and the routine of Juan setting up a schedule. By doing this, Juan had taken the choice out of Ellen's Locus of Control.

With that knowledge, Juan and I had a conversation with Ellen. It seems that Ellen had difficulty getting her kids off to school and had a transportation issue because she rode the bus to the office. I asked Ellen, "*What time would be convenient for you to start work? By convenient, I mean a time that would allow you to show up here on time every day, with no instances of being late.*" Ellen seemed to feel that she could get to work on time if she started at 8:00 AM instead of 7:00 AM. I then went on to ask Ellen, "*If we were to allow you the choice of starting at 8:00 AM instead of 7:00 AM and you came in late, what should happen to you?*" She replied, "*I should be fired.*"

However, Juan didn't have the authority to fire Ellen for being late one time, so we had to help Ellen come up with a realistic set of consequences—consequences that she chose.

Juan, of course, had some issues with this employee-directed approach. His first response was that he was the boss and it is the boss that sets the schedule, not the employees. "*If we let Ellen set her own schedule, all the others will want to do it too. It will be chaos.*" Of course, the reality is most employees don't want to think about having to set their own schedule. They like the certainty of a routine set up for them by someone else. But even if they did, wouldn't it be worth the extra effort that it would cause in scheduling if you could positively influence the motivation of that worker? Too often an organization controls showing up to the point where their workers get the message that the only thing that is important is showing up. After they clock in, they feel like they have succeeded for the day. It creates what military folks like to refer to as ROAD warriors (retired on active duty).

Juan was stuck in a power and control issue. If he gave Ellen the power and control to choose her start time, he viewed it as losing something—moving it out of his Locus of Control. I pointed out to Juan that we had begun the whole discussion because Ellen was coming in late. In other words her behavior of coming late was already out of his Locus of Control. He didn't determine what time Ellen came to work by the schedule he set. She determined what time she started work by what time she showed up. All we were doing was admitting that reality and making certain that Ellen owned the fact that showing up on time was clearly in her Locus of Control.

Still, Juan was not prepared to give in to this line of thinking entirely. He did agree, however, to allow Ellen to try it as a pilot test. After nine months of Ellen showing up on time, Juan finally made it permanent.

Case Study: Micromanaging Clyde

Another good example is Clyde. Clyde was referred for coaching because he was having difficulty meeting productivity standards in his position. During the first coaching appointment, I asked Clyde why he thought he was having difficulty meeting the standard. His reply came clearly and quickly. *"I can't meet targets because my boss Samantha over-controls my workload."* When prompted for clarification, Clyde explained more fully.

Samantha brings me the work one piece at a time. Sometimes, I am sitting there with almost nothing to do. Other times, I have a pile of work so large that I can't see over my desk to the person in front of me. Also, she is in meetings all morning and typically only brings work over after lunch. That makes my workload very light in the morning and really heavy in the afternoon. If you really thought about the work-flow, it doesn't make sense for the work to flow through her desk at all. Operations could really just drop the stuff to me directly.

When I contacted Samantha to explore why she controlled the work assignments the way she did, she said it was because she didn't think her people could make good decisions about timing the workflow and that she needed to do that for them. She managed a group of eleven people. I shared with her, with Clyde's permission, what he had told me about his feelings about her approach. I also volunteered to explore this with the other ten people in her group. Nine of the ten felt the same way Clyde did. Armed with that information, I approached Samantha again and asked her if she would be willing to consider a pilot test that would change the way the workload was assigned. She agreed to a four-week test of a system that would allow Operations to bring the work directly to her people and let them schedule their own approach to getting that work done.

At the end of the four weeks, the average turnaround time for work in her group had been reduced by 24 hours and the average cycle time to complete the work had fallen. As a bonus, her team had identified a new area of service that they could provide to Operations without any additional staff.

Broadening the Scope of Choices

Broadening the scope of the choices means allowing an individual to make choices about areas of work that heretofore had been controlled by another person.

Case Study: Ellen Works From Home

Let's go back to Juan and Ellen for a good example of broadening the scope of choices. After nine months of success, I asked Juan if he would be willing to try an experiment that would allow Ellen to work at home. *"Absolutely not,"* he quickly replied. *"How would I know she was working?"* When I asked how he knew she was working now, he smiled and said, *"because I can see her when she is at her desk."*

Of course, that only meant he could see her looking like she was working. It didn't mean she was actually contributing productively or adding value to the organization's customers. Managers often confuse this ability to look busy with an employee actively adding value to the organization. It is the type of management thinking that stimulates employees to design computer keyboard shortcuts to switch from a web browser to a spreadsheet when the boss walks by.

Managers often get bogged down in maintaining the illusion of control to the point where they negatively impact a worker's willingness to actively engage. In the context of the Motivational Grid, they move things from the worker's Locus of Control to an external position. That puts it into either the Fear or Apathy quadrant, as illustrated in **Fig. 6.1**. So, a manager has to either manage by fear, or emotionally brow beat the apathetic worker to keep them on task. Is that the way you want to manage?

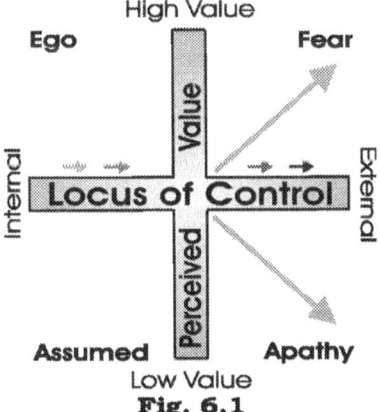

Fig. 6.1

By allowing Ellen the choice to work at home, the choice becomes not just to show up physically, but to show up emotionally and psychologically as well. It also sends Ellen the signal that she is trusted, which increases her feelings of self-efficacy and psychological integration. That makes the Pay Value higher and more immediate for her.

There are many other examples of the management tendency towards the illusion of control leading to a de-motivational environment.

Case Study: Evelyn's Phone Upgrade

Evelyn is another good example. Evelyn worked as an outside service representative. She traveled all over the United States working with her organization's customers. One day, Evelyn came into her coaching session looking very downtrodden. She was usually bubbly and upbeat, so I asked her what was wrong. She started pouring it out:

This company really doesn't value me at all. I work my ass off for them and all they give me back is grief. I am out on the road 15 to 20 days a month, but these bureaucrats at the home office don't get it how hard that is. I requested an upgrade for my cell phone because the one I have won't hold enough numbers in memory. They told me that reps only get the 160 phone and if I wanted an upgrade I would have to pay for it myself. Of course, the damn VPs that hardly ever travel get the upgrade. Hell, they hardly ever use their damn phones except to call their wives. Why should I have to pay for the upgrade that I need to supply good service to our customers? I guess I'll just pay the upgrade and pad my expense report to cover the costs. I hate doing that, because it really doesn't fit with my values. It's like lying. But I'll be damned if I am going to spend my money on this upgrade!

Evelyn's tirade illustrated a number of issues we touched on already. Her motivation was to serve the customer, but she didn't feel like the company was supporting her in this. She felt that the company was taking away her choice. They were moving her Locus of Control by saying she couldn't determine what type of phone she needed. She had already developed a strategy to move the Locus of Control back into her realm. However, that decision was grating on her because it didn't fit with her own values. It was negatively impacting her psychological integration. Notice that she doesn't consider, at least not yet, downgrading the service to her customers. That would negatively impact her psychological and social integration. I predict, however, if Evelyn has many more interactions like this with management, she will start to disengage and her productivity and quality will decline.

Clarifying the Choices

Obviously, that wasn't the first situation where Evelyn had experienced a negative impact of the unthinking application of organizational policy. However, she was at a crossroads. She was talking about crossing an ethical line. It was time to help Evelyn clarify her choices.

"*Is padding your expense report the only way you can get what you need here?*" I asked.

"*Yes, it's the only way I see.*"

As I continued to probe, Evelyn was able to see that she could enlist the support of her boss and her boss's boss. She also had a good relationship with the VP of Operations and could lobby for his support. In other words, it became clear to her that she had other options that she could choose.

We then went on to explore the ramifications of her choosing to pad her expense report. Evelyn was able to identify the negative impact it would have on her psychological integration because she would feel like a slimeball. She was also able to identify a negative impact on her social integration because she wouldn't be able to talk about that with others at work. It would be a dirty little secret that she would have to keep and would make her feel isolated from her co-workers. Finally, she was able to admit to herself that there was at least a small possibility that she would be exposed as a cheater and might lose her job. The combination of identifying other options for her choice and clarifying the ramifications of the one option she was considering allowed Evelyn to move forward in a more constructive way. Because she took the time to work through the decision, it also allowed her to increase her feelings of self-efficacy, increasing her motivation.

Summary: Managing Locus of Control

Increase the Number of Choices

- Timing of work

- Order of work

- Location of work

- Nature of the work

Broaden the Scope of Choices

- Take on more responsibility

- Take on different responsibility

- Keep the Locus of Control with employee

Clarify the Choices

- Help employee identify choice criteria

- Help employee clarify potential choices

- Help employee evaluate ramifications of potential choices

- Recognize your own issues in allowing employee choice

7

Focusing on Strengths

There is a school of psychological thought that asserts that the best way to stimulate behavioral change is to focus on the strengths that an individual exhibits rather than focusing on their perceived shortcomings. This approach is known as the Strengths Based Perspective. Manager's can benefit from this same mode of thinking when trying to influence an employee's motivational determinants. In most cases, strengths and weaknesses are situational. In other words, behavior that might be considered a strength in one situation might be considered a weakness in another set of circumstances. For instance, an employee that is wordy and takes a long time to explain any point may be considered overbearing and inconsiderate in a team meeting. That same employee might be highly suited for writing a manual or presenting training material. Or, an employee that always questions instructions might be considered difficult in a meeting where a manager is merely dispensing information but be an excellent person to involve in problem solving meetings.

The key for the manager is to have the ability to discover an employee's strengths and then be able to engage the employee in assignments that take advantage of those strengths. There are a number of business-oriented strength dichotomies that a manager may want to consider as they evaluate each employee.

Internal Focus vs. External Focus

Individuals with an internal focus tend to gather information and ideas by taking them in, processing them within themselves, before being prepared to make judgements, conclusions, and observations to others. These folks will want to chew on it alone. They work well on individual projects. Externally focused individuals, on the other hand, tend to process information and ideas by putting them out to others. They will want to talk about information and ideas with others. Externals work well in team environments, particularly in the early stages of a project when you want to solicit a lot of involvement, get ideas, and consider different points of view. They are also excellent choices when you want to get the word out about a new program or idea.

Inductive vs. Deductive

People with an inductive orientation tend to start with the facts and build conclusions after taking in a lot of sensory information. Those with a deductive approach tend to start with an idea and then fill in the details that fit that idea. An inductive orientation is well suited for tasks such as information gathering, root cause analysis, and process mapping. Individuals with an inductive orientation tend be more aware of sensory input and will notice details that others might miss.

An individual with a deductive orientation will tend to create a hypothesis that captures the big picture and then see an application to that in many places. People with a deductive orientation seem well suited for developing scenarios to be used in planning. They are excited and engaged while developing a mission or vision statement. If combined with an external orientation, they tend to be natural leaders that get others excited about the possibilities of what can be done. It may be necessary to balance this individual with an inductive person who offers a few yes buts to help keep the deductive/external grounded in reality.

Values vs. Rules

Some individuals are focused on values or precognitive commitments about what is important or the way the world should be. When people with this type of orientation rise to the top of organizations, they typically put those values at the forefront of their management effort. They stress things like integrity, honesty, and fairness, not necessarily because they feel it gives the organization an advantage in the market place, but because it is the right thing to do. Their value-based beliefs drive behavior. People with a value-based orientation tend to do well in environments where there is rapid change and a loose structure. They use those values to help steer through the change and see order among what others may see as chaos.

Of course, not everyone who has this value orientation is in top management. Many people operate from this preference. As a manager, if I do not recognize this and tap into it, not only am I missing an opportunity, but also I may be stimulating problems with productivity and quality.

At the other side of this dichotomy is a rule-based preference. Individuals with this preference want operating guidelines and boundaries laid out clearly. You may hear them say something like "just tell me what you want me to do and I'll do it." They will make frequent reference to policy, procedure, and instructions. If none exist, they are the ideal folks to put in charge of creating them. People with a rule-based preference tend to do well and blossom in environments that are stable and structured.

Task vs. Relationship

People with a clear task preference want to roll up their sleeves, get down to brass tacks, and get the job at hand done. They are great people to turn to when the pressure is on, a threat is imminent, or timeframes are short. They will overcome obstacles, organize resources, and get things moving.

People with a relationship preference tend to get to know everyone. They will try to make certain that everyone is comfortable with a group decision. They will usually be able to tell you how other people in the work group feel about a subject. They will also likely know what is going on with other people both at work and at home.

Process vs. Outcomes

An individual with a clear process preference will naturally see how the individual parts of a task fit into a flow to create an outcome. They also see how those tasks fit together to create value to a customer. They can diagram a workflow and see meaning in it the way most of us see meaning in a roadmap. People with this preference make strong contributions to bringing order to the workplace, spotting inefficiencies, and building systems to keep things on track.

An individual with a preference towards outcomes is great at getting things done. They drive towards the desired result, sometimes bending (or completely ignoring) policy, procedures, or rules. They tend to believe that the ends justify the means.

Structure vs. Adaptability

Individuals with a preference for structure like to superimpose order on a set of tasks or a group of people. These individuals shine if the organization needs to create procedures, define reporting, or set up a communication framework. When a chain of command isn't present, they will try to (or at least want to) create one.

Individuals with a preference for adaptability, on the other hand, will keep things loose and free flowing. They tend to stand out and perform well in environments where there is rapid change or weakly defined inter-relationships. They fit in quickly in a new environment.

I am sure there are many other strength dichotomies. This list is certainly not exhaustive. I offer it here merely to get you thinking about what strengths you may see in your people. A great resource for this is the book, *Now Discover Your Strengths*, by Marcus Buckingham and Curt Coffman.

Summary: Focusing on Strengths

A key role for a manager is to discover and engage an employee's strengths.

Strengths and weaknesses are situational. A weakness in one situation can be a strength in another context.

There are a number of strength dichotomies a manager should be aware of:

- Internal vs. External Focus
- Inductive vs. Deductive Thinking
- Values vs. Rules
- Task vs. Relationship
- Process vs. Outcomes
- Structure vs. Adaptability

8

The Restructuring Cycle

An Overview

Cognitive Restructuring is a systematic approach to changing the way an individual perceives or frames a set of facts or circumstance.

Therapists and counselors have used Cognitive Restructuring for a long time as a tool for positive behavioral change. So managers don't have to reinvent the wheel to learn effective techniques to influence their employees. There is already a well-defined and validated process to use. This process is called the Restructuring Cycle. The Cycle has four phases: Identification, Options, Practice, and Habituation, as illustrated in **Fig. 8.1**.

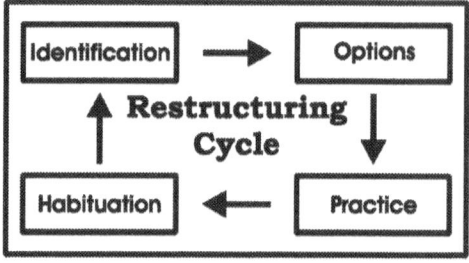

Fig. 8.1

One of the frustrating facts for a manager to deal with is that an individual's motivation is heavily influenced by their beliefs, such as the employee's beliefs about their potential, abilities and the way the world works. It would be so neat and tidy if these beliefs were based upon rational thinking and logic. Reality is much messier. Many of an employee's beliefs may be far from rational. Their belief system can be filled with thoughts that cause their view of themselves and the world to be off base from the reality that those around them observe.

As a manager, you should be able to recognize thought patterns that may require your intervention to help an employee move forward. These thought patterns are often referred to as cognitive distortions. It is typically very difficult for an individual to recognize and change these cognitive distortions on their own. They need another pair of eyes and ears to observe behavioral patterns and listen to conversation to spot the signs of these distortions. Since it is so difficult to spot your own distorted thinking, the first place a manager should start is to seek out the help of a coach, mentor, or peer group to recognize his or her own cognitive distortions.

Here are some common cognitive distortions that are likely targets for the application of the Restructuring Cycle:

Targets for the Restructuring Cycle

Perfectionism

Perfectionism is the pattern of setting unrealistically high expectations for performance on one's self and others. When a person does this, it leads them to frequently fall short of goals and undermines their own or other's sense of self-efficacy. It may also lead to a high fear of failure that grows into a low tolerance for risk. They start to play is safe all the time.

Catastrophizing

Catastrophizing means making things seem a great deal worse than they are in reality. For instance, a worker that is concerned about potential negative feedback from their boss may believe they will be fired if they make even a small mistake.

Fairness Fallacy

The Fairness Fallacy means falsely assuming a certain favorable treatment will be given. This expected treatment is defined as fair. People stymied by this distortion complain that another individual, or a set of circumstances, or life in general isn't fair. Typically, it means that they perceive someone or something has some advantage over them due to some mysterious force that they have no way to overcome.

Blaming

Blaming means attributing results to a force outside of oneself, typically in such a way as to make it seem that the person doing the blaming cannot be held accountable. In the context of the Motivational Vector Grid, an individual struggling under this cognitive distortion would push the Locus of Control towards the external side of the scale, even though it might be something that others, who were more objective, would say is well within that individual's Locus of Control.

Polarized Thinking

Polarized Thinking means only seeing two options, at extreme opposites from each other, rather than a broad range of alternatives that are actually possible. People dealing with this distortion separate their options into two mutually exclusive categories; you are either with them or against them; it is either good or bad. The answer is either yes or no. In most situations, there is a range of options between the two extremes that goes unrecognized by someone caught in this cognitive trap.

We can find many examples of this in the world. The epidemic of eating disorders in teens is a manifestation of how cognitive distortions can impact behavior in a negative way. In the business environment, the following case study shows a widely held cognitive distortion about the work ethic of younger workers.

Case Study: John and These Kids Today!

John supervised a team of customer service representatives. Most of his employees were 20 somethings, new to the work-world. In a group coaching session, John began to talk about his relationship to his team:

These kids are different than the folks I started work with. They just don't have a work ethic anymore. They view it as just a job. They don't want to put out any extra effort. They will do what they're told, but you constantly have to nudge them. It wasn't like that when I started to work. I wanted to make an impression on the boss. I was constantly looking for ways to show my boss that I could excel and that I wanted to accept extra responsibility.

As John's peer coaching group started to probe into this situation, a completely different picture started to come into focus. It seems that John's company had done quite a bit of work to recruit, train, and retain these young people for their workforce. As part of that effort, they had done surveys and focus groups with young people to discover what they were looking for in a work environment. Three things were clearly identified from that effort:

- A chance to participate in making decisions (high Locus of Control).

- A company that would return their loyalty and efforts by creating a secure and stable work situation (Locus of Control and Pay Value).

- An opportunity to be paid superior wages for superior performance (Pay Value).

The peer group, when they discovered this, was on John like a cheap suit. They wanted to know how John could square his opinion that his workers had no work ethic with the information the company had discovered in their surveys and focus groups. One of his peers summarized the feelings of the group succinctly when she said: *"It sounds to me like those kids have a very strong work ethic, so it doesn't seem like the problem is with that."*

As the dialogue developed in the group, it turned out that John had made little effort to involve the young workers in decision making. There was only a two-percent spread in their pay system between the average and superior performers at evaluation time. The group also dug out that the company had experienced three large layoffs in the past five years—sending a message to the workforce that the company did not value loyalty with a reciprocal commitment. In other words, the group pointed out to John that this was a management problem, not a problem with his young employees' work ethic.

In the context of the Motivational Vector Grid, John had put this situation as a low Locus of Control for him by blaming the young employees' work ethic. Their work ethic was something he perceived that he had little control over. When his coaching group pointed out that he had almost complete control over how much he involved his team in decision making, John was able to make positive changes in his management style. In other words, the group had helped John complete a Cognitive Restructuring in the way he perceived

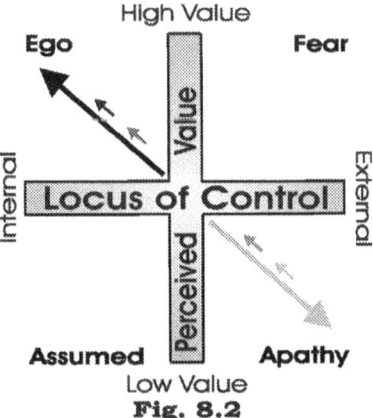

Fig. 8.2

the challenge he was facing. They had helped him shift his beliefs on the Locus of Control axis so he could move from the Apathy Quadrant to the Ego Quadrant in his approach, as illustrated in **Fig 8.2**.

Summary: Restructuring Cycle Overview

Cognitive Restructuring is a systematic approach to changing the way an individual perceives or frames a set of facts or circumstances.

The **Restructuring Cycle** is an organized approach to helping an individual complete a Cognitive Restructuring.

The Restructuring Cycle has four phases:

- **Identification** of the thought pattern to be changed
- Developing and evaluating **Options** an individual might consider
- Provide a safe environment to **Practice** the new thinking or behavior
- **Habituation** of the new pattern into daily routine

Common cognitive distortions that are good targets for the Restructuring Cycle:

- **Perfectionism**: setting unrealistically high expectations
- **Catastrophizing**: making things seem much worse than they are
- **Fairness Fallacy**: falsely assuming that some preconceived treatment (the fair treatment in the individual's mind) will be given
- **Blaming**: attributing results to a force outside of self to absolve oneself of responsibility
- **Polarized Thinking**: seeing only two options, at extreme opposites from each other, rather than a broad range of possibilities

9

Identification Phase of the Restructuring Cycle

Since changing the way an employee thinks is critical to a manager's success in changing behavior, it is important to know how to use the Restructuring Cycle. In this chapter, we'll begin a detailed example that works through all four phases of the Restructuring Cycle: Identification, Options, Practice, and Habituation.

The Identification Phase of the Restructuring Cycle is an exploratory phase to help the individual check their current state. When helping an individual through this phase, a manager wants to help them identify their current thoughts, feelings, and behaviors. The goal is to help the individual clarify what they are thinking, feeling, and doing. So the manager wants to explore these three major areas: intellectual activity, emotional activity, and behavioral activity.

For now, we are going to assume that the employee we are working with understands and acknowledges that their current behavior needs to change. If that is not the case, you many want to use *Envisioning the Future* explained in detail in Chapter 12 to help them motivate themselves to change.

The easiest place to start is with the intellectual activity—what the employee is thinking. For most people this will be the least threatening area to talk about. Typically, this dialogue will begin with a question such as: "I'm sure that you had some good thoughts that stimulated you to do that. Would you mind sharing them with me?"

Notice that the statement that precedes the question builds a sense of self-efficacy. Also, the question itself implies that the Locus of Control is clearly with the employee. They have a choice to share their thoughts or not.

Let's look at a dialogue between a manager and her direct report to see how this might sound.

Case Study: Georgina's Customer Site Visits

Georgina, a staff consultant, had established a track record of an average trip length of four days to provide service to her clients. The other six consultants in her group averaged only half that time to provide service to a similar client base in the same geographic area. Her manager, Karen, while reviewing the end of year statistics and financial reports had noticed this difference. Karen's first response was to check the customer service feedback and performance information from the client's Georgina served. She wanted to see if she could see if there were any differences that would explain why Georgina needed twice as long, on average, to service her client's requests. Karen even went so far as to research the records from a previous time when another consultant had serviced the same accounts to determine if that consultant had also had a longer average trip length. The previous consultant had averaged two days for the same client base.

Prepared with that information, Karen decided to approach Georgina to see if she could motivate her to reduce the average length of her trips. She made an appointment to speak with Georgina in private the following Monday.

Karen: *Thanks for coming in today. I know how busy you are and how demanding it is to provide service to your clients. I appreciate you carving out time to meet with me. As I mentioned to you on the phone, I'm trying to better understand what factors influence how long it takes to provide service to our customers. I see from my reports that your average trip length is four days. I'd like to ask you some questions to help me understand how you plan for trips and how you evaluate how long you stay. When you are planning your trips, what things go through your mind to try to estimate how long you will need to stay?*

Georgina: *Well, I like to consider the service record, so I check our call history. I also like to think about how complex the problem is I'll be working on with them. I consider how many people and work teams I will need to meet with so I can get a feel for scheduling those. I know it's expensive to make these on-site service visits so I want to make sure I am thorough and get it all done the first time out so I don't have to go back.*

Karen: *So you place a high value on prior planning and on making sure you include everyone on the client site?*

Georgina: *Absolutely. I want to be thought of as the most customer friendly and responsive person on our team.*

Karen: *So you feel that it is important to take as much time as you need to satisfy that client's needs?*

Georgina: *For sure.*

Karen: *It sounds like you are quite proud of the level of service you provide our clients.*

Georgina: *Yes, I feel like I go out of my way to do the best I can for them and it makes me feel really good that they respond positively to my efforts.*

Notice that Karen makes no judgement as she discusses this with Georgina. That's important at this early stage of the process.

During the Identification Phase, a manager should probe to understand what's going on with the employee in the three key areas of thoughts, feelings, and behavior.

Many managers have difficulty with the area of feelings. In a business culture, managers are often given the message that feelings are unimportant and it is not appropriate to discuss feelings in the work environment. Feelings are considered as personal and, as such, off limits for managers to explore. "Leave your personal life at the door" is a management mantra in many organizations.

But for Restructuring Cycle, it is critical for the manager to understand the feeling component of behavior. There are three areas to probe: physiological, emotional, and value congruence. Congruence means that one thing is in harmony or goes along with another. If someone is having a performance problem, or if their behavior doesn't match their values and beliefs, it may show up in physical sensations in the body. On some level they may be aware that their belief or behavior is counter-intentional to their desired ends. This uneasiness manifest itself in physical sensations and we say they are not physiologically congruent. The individual can also lack congruence in their values. For instance, if I want to produce a quality outcome, but load myself up with too much work to devote the proper attention to a report, I may lack congruence between two values (producing quality work and producing a high quantity of work). There can also be a problem with emotional congruence. For instance, if a worker wants to be promoted, but doesn't want to hold their former co-workers accountable for meeting deadlines or budgets it could cause emotional incongruence.

In the conversation between Georgina and Karen, Karen has, up to this point, focused on learning Georgina's values. Let's go back to their conversation and see how Karen probes to uncover Georgina's feelings.

Karen: *It's admirable that you take the time to scope out the client's needs and to identify all the players in their organization that you will need to work with. I am also impressed that you show consideration for minimizing the costs to our company by trying to meet all their needs in one trip. That shows intelligence as well as a strong value for customer service. It also shows a strong sense of the business imperative we face to manage our costs. Listening to you, however, I get the feeling that your preparations put you under a great deal of stress. It almost sounds like you are anxious, almost fearful. Am I reading your emotions correctly?*

Georgina: *Well, I am certainly anxious, although I wouldn't go so far as to call it fear. I do sometimes feel afraid that if I miss something the client will feel I am incompetent.*

Karen: *Has that happened to you before?*

Georgina: *Yes. Several years ago I made a trip and didn't prepare the way I do now. I really blew the visit and the client complained to my manager. It was before your time, but I still remember it like it was yesterday.*

Karen: *Wow, having that memory so clear in your mind must make you really nervous. I know when I have feelings like that my heart races, my pulse gets rapid, and I start perspiring. Do you have that kind of reaction too?*

Georgina: *Absolutely. I have to use a checklist that I have developed to make sure I don't miss anything.*

Karen: *That's a great idea to help you manage the stress. Can you let me see a copy of that?*

Notice how Karen focuses on Georgina's strengths throughout the conversation. She takes every opportunity to build Georgina's sense of self-efficacy. She also begins to identify Georgina's psychological process of managing the situation. Georgina also begins to identify the behavior (following a checklist) that results from her process.

Let's look at what's happening on the surface here. Georgina is using a very comprehensive, detailed approach to planning and executing her customer visits. Ostensibly, the purpose of her process is to provide top-notch service while managing the costs to her company by making certain she does it right the first time. She seems proud of the level of service she is providing and comfortable that she is doing a good job. How could any manager fault Georgina for that approach? In reality, Karen knows that other representatives are achieving similar results in half the service time.

During her dialogue with Georgina, however, Karen has uncovered a Motivational Vector that has been influencing Georgina's performance. So let's examine the Motivational Vectors on Georgina's Grid. There is one for her stated desire to provide good service to her customers. There is a second for her stated desire to help the company manage costs. There is a third Vector that represents the newly uncovered desire to avoid negative feedback because she missed something.

So at this point, her Motivational Vector Grid looks something like the illustration **Fig. 9.1.**

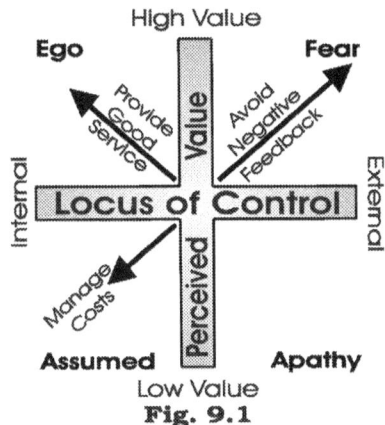

Fig. 9.1

Georgina feels there is a high Perceived Value to rendering good customer service. She has structured her service delivery so that delivering that good service is well within her Locus of Control. So her Motivational Vector, labeled *Provide Good Service*, is clearly in the Ego Quadrant.

She has a low Perceived Value for managing costs, partially because she hasn't received sufficient formative feedback to know her performance in this area is unacceptable. Because she has heard no negative feedback, she feels her ability to manage costs is still well within her Locus of Control. That places her Motivational Vector to manage costs clearly in the Assumed Quadrant.

Finally, Karen has uncovered another factor (Georgina's aversion to negative feedback) that has high Perceived Value. While it may seem to Georgina that she has this in an internal Locus of Control, it should be obvious to Karen at this point that it is clearly out of control. So the external Locus of Control and a high Pay Value puts this Motivational Vector in the Fear Quadrant.

A typical response to this situation might be for Karen to share all the data she has collected with Georgina and force her to set targets to reduce her average trip to two days. That would shift the *Manage Costs* Motivational Vector from the Assumed to the Fear Quadrant. Unfortunately, it is also likely to move the *Provide Good Service* Motivational Vector from the Ego Quadrant to either the Assumed or Apathy Quadrant. In other words, Georgina is likely to sacrifice quality for the sake of cost management. That would be an undesirable outcome for Georgina, Karen, the company, and the clients.

Karen needs to find some way to raise the Pay Value for the Manage Cost Motivational Vector while at the same time lowering either the Pay Value or Locus of Control for the Avoid Negative Feedback Motivational Vector. This brings Karen to the next phase of the Restructuring Cycle, Options.

Summary: Restructuring Cycle Identification Phase

First phase of the Restructuring Cycle, which includes four phases: Identification, Options, Practice, and Habituation.

An exploratory phase for the individual to check their current state

- What is the employee thinking?
- What is the employee feeling?
  - Is there physiological congruence?
  - Is their emotional congruence?
  - Is there value congruence?
- How is the employee behaving?

Used with employees that acknowledge that current behavior needs to change

Always build from the employee's strengths

10

Options Phase of the Restructuring Cycle

The purpose of the Options Phase of the Restructuring Cycle is fourfold:

1. To help an individual clarify their desired outcomes

2. To identify and own their thinking and behavior

3. To generate as many alternatives as possible

4. To recognize the Pay Value that may come from a change in behavior

The Options Phase is a divergent phase that fosters and supports creative thinking.

Case Study: Georgina's Customer Site Visits (Continued)

Karen, through her dialogue with Georgina has uncovered a counter-intentional thought (If I don't plan and execute every trip perfectly, I am going to get in trouble). Having discovered that, she can now move the dialogue into the Options Phase. During this phase, Karen has four objectives. First, to clarify and have Georgina own her intentionality. Second, to help Georgina recognize the counter-intentional thoughts and the counter-intentional behavior that results. Third, to guide Georgina as she researches and develops alternatives. Fourth, to help Georgina identify the Pay Value to modifying her thoughts and behavior.

Notice that Georgina's thoughts and behaviors are not framed as irrational or dysfunctional. We don't want to make them wrong. The term counter-intentional reflects that human behavior, for the most part, is stimulated by intentionality. We act in a certain way because we believe, either consciously or unconsciously, that the behavior will lead to an outcome we want. In short, we behave in a certain way because we intend for a certain response or expect a particular result. So it is fair to call behavior intentional.

Unfortunately, our behavior doesn't always give us the response or result that we intended. Hence, we use the term counter-intentional to indicate a behavior that doesn't result in the outcome an individual intended.

Let's listen in as Karen continues the dialogue with Georgina:

Karen: *So Georgina, I hear a number of outcomes you intend to achieve from the process you use to plan and conduct your customer visits. One outcome is to provide good customer service to your customers. Another outcome is to try to make certain that you cover all your bases with the first visit. Still another is a desire to avoid potentially negative feedback from the customer and me as your boss. The final one I heard is that you want to help the company manage its overall cost of supplying customer service. Does that sum it up?*

Georgina: *Yes, that's about it.*

Karen: *Let's write those down so I can keep them clearly in mind. (Karen writes them). So Georgina, of these four outcomes that you intend to realize, which would you say is most important to you?*

Georgina: *Of course the most important is providing good customer service and controlling our costs. I would put them as number one and number two.*

Karen: *I know if my boss asked me to rank these, I would put those two first right away. But I think if I thought about it honestly to myself, the thing I would put at the top is avoiding the negative feedback. I would like you to take a minute to think about this and consider where that one really ranks for you. (Karen sits quietly)*

Georgina: *(Hesitantly), Well, I would have to say that is quite important to me. I would have to put it near the top. I still think the customer service is most important but I would have to say avoiding the criticism would be a strong second for me.*

Karen: *Okay, so the desire to provide good customer service is number one, avoiding the potential for negative criticism is number two, and the cost management would be number three for you?*

Georgina: *Well, actually no. I would have to put covering all my bases above that.*

Karen: *Okay then. I have to make an observation at this point Georgina. When we were talking earlier, I got the clear impression that a significant part of your motivation for giving good customer service and making sure you covered all your bases was the concern you have about avoiding the potential for negative criticism. Did I read that right?*

Georgina: *Well, I want to do a good job because it makes me feel good. But, yes, a part of what makes it important to me is I don't ever want to get bawled out like that again.*

Karen: *I understand completely. Given your earlier experience, I think I would be cautious as well. I wonder, however, if perhaps you aren't overemphasizing that past experience and overcompensating just a bit. Have you ever seen, or heard of, me treating any of the service reps the way the former supervisor treated you?*

Georgina: *No. I think you are very supportive of all of us.*

Karen: *Thank you. I appreciate that positive feedback and want to assure you that I would never be abusive of you. I don't expect our people to be perfect. I make mistakes and have oversights that lead to problems and I know our reps will as well. What I want is for all of us to learn from that so we can, over time, improve our performance. Do you agree that oversights and errors can be a wonderful opportunity for us to learn and improve?*

Georgina: *Yes, I would like to think that I learn from my mistakes.*

Karen: *You obviously do. Think about how you have improved your process for planning these trips and the checklist you developed.*

Georgina: *Yes, I suppose that's true.*

Karen: *I would like to use that talent in a new way. I want you to see if you can improve your process in a way to reduce your average trip time from four days. I would like you to help me with this project to examine how people plan and execute their visits. Can you interview the other reps and prepare a report that compares your process and results to theirs?*

Georgina: *Of course, if you think it would be helpful. I could do that.*

Karen: *Great, I really appreciate your willingness to bring your talents to this project. I have some data that I have gathered already on average trip length, results of the satisfaction surveys, and return trips that will help jump-start the effort. But I want to look behind the raw numbers to consider the process each rep uses and then compare their results and their processes to see what we can learn from that.*

Georgina: *(Taking the papers) Okay, I'll get right on it. When do you want it?*

Karen: *Well, since you'll be fitting this in around your other work, I would like you to give me an idea of when you feel you can have it done.*

Georgina: *Well, I think I can do it within two weeks. Is that soon enough?*

Karen: *That will be fine. I really appreciate your willingness to take this on. Thanks for your good work and for the focus you have on serving our customers.*

Georgina: *Okay, then. Bye.*

With that, Karen has set Georgina off on a path of self-discovery to start to research and formulate alternatives. That is the next step in the Options Phase.

Notice that Karen is using Georgina's natural strengths and applying them to the challenge at hand. Notice also that Karen is leaving the action clearly in Georgina's Locus of Control. By providing lots of positive feedback, Karen is also capitalizing on something that Georgina has already identified as a high Pay Value for her. So in terms of the Motivational Vector Grid, Karen is supporting Georgina in a way that keeps her firmly in the Ego Quadrant.

Let's listen in as Karen processes the results of Georgina's research to help her identify alternatives.

Karen: *Well, let's review what you've found. I'd like to start with the data I provided you. What did you make of that?*

Georgina: *That was really interesting to me. I thought that all the planning and worrying I do would show up in dramatically different results on the customer surveys, but most of the reps do as well or better than I do in the customer satisfaction surveys. Yet, they have an average trip length of half of mine and no more re-service trips. It really opened my eyes and showed me that there must be different ways to get the same results. It made me anxious to interview each of them to compare what they did to what I did.*

Karen: *That's exciting to hear that you found useful information in that data. Sometimes I worry that we collect all these facts and never are able to make any practical use of them. I'm glad you found them helpful. What did you find when you interviewed the other reps?*

Georgina: *Well, there are a lot of similarities in what we do. We all prepare in pretty much the same way. The difference comes in the way we handle the on-site meetings.*

Karen: *Oh, how's that?*

Georgina: *Well, I am the only one that schedules direct meetings with the second level people. All the other reps coach the first level people on how to conduct those meetings with the second level people, but let the client's folks actually do the meetings. This not only saves them a lot of time, but the first level people seem to like it. It makes them feel more in control, I suppose. It's a great idea. If I did that, I could substantially reduce my time on site.*

Karen: *Yes, it does seem like an idea that might be worth testing. Would you want to do that?*

Georgina: *Yes, I would.*

Karen: *How do you think you might prepare yourself for that?*

Georgina: *Well, John and Marie both do it and I like them a lot. I could ask them to coach me to get me ready.*

Karen: *Is there anything I can do to help with that?*

Georgina: *Yes, could you arrange some special reward for them for helping me?*

Karen: *I would be willing to try. Why don't you explore with them what they might consider a suitable reward and get back to me?*

Georgina: *Okay.*

The next step in the Options Phase is to help the individual identify the Pay Values associated with successfully performing the new behaviors. There are two levels of behavioral accomplishment: Doing and Being. In making a change, an individual may need to take small steps by doing things differently before they can reach the desired set of behavioral routines or states of being. For instance, if I want to lose 25 pounds (Being goal), I may need to stop eating Ben and Jerry's ice cream every night (Doing goal). When helping an individual identify Pay Values, it is important to have them think of the Pay Values for both Being and Doing goals.

Let's listen in as Karen works with Georgina to identify the Being and Doing Pay Values for her change.

Karen: *Well, it sounds like you have John and Marie on board for your practice. That's great.*

Georgina: *Yea, I appreciate your willingness to let them go to that seminar as a reward. They probably would have done it without that, but it was definitely something they appreciated.*

Karen: *This is going to be a significant change for you. If you're like me, that kind of uncertainty is a bit scary. Let me ask you this: What do you think you'll get out of this? What are the benefits to you of making this change?*

Georgina: *Well, I do think it will improve my ratings on my annual evaluation, but those are already pretty good so that's not a big deal to me. I think it will, however, make a big improvement with the first level managers at some of my key clients.*

Karen: *Oh, which ones?*

Georgina: *Well, I think the folks at Fox Systems are going to love this approach. Also, the people over at Caratene will eat it up. Best of all for me, the people at ZeePoint. They are my toughest account and I always feel like I am struggling with them. I think this approach will make it much easier.*

Karen: *Great. In addition to improving your relationship with those key accounts, what else will this change give you?*

Georgina: *Well, this might sound a bit silly, but it will make me feel better about myself. I will feel like I am a better rep if I can do this successfully.*

Karen: *No, that doesn't sound silly to me at all. I value my feelings about how well I perform and can understand perfectly why this will be important to you. Is there anything else?*

Georgina: *Well, yes. You know how I told you about wanting to avoid negative criticism? Well, I think this will not only avoid the negative, but also get me a lot of positive recognition as well.*

Karen: *Yes, I can see that. I can assure you that I will want to give you a lot of feedback. In fact, I was thinking about writing up your experience in the company newspaper. It would be a positive example of self-directed continual improvement. That would get you company-wide recognition. Would you like that?*

Georgina: *Wow, I never thought about that. I'm not sure how that would feel. Can I think about it and get back to you?*

Karen: *Of course.*

To this point, Karen has only been focused on the Being Pay Values, in other words the goodies Georgina will get if she successfully makes the change. Let's listen in again as Karen moves on to helping Georgina identify Doing Pay Values.

Karen: *Of course, Georgina, you have some work to do along the way to reach these Pay Values we have been discussing. There's a lot of time and effort between here and there. Let's think a little bit about the Pay Values that you are going to have along the way. What pluses do you see to the practice you will be doing with John and Marie?*

Georgina: *Hmm. I never thought about that—having Pay Values from the practice I'll be doing. One thing that comes to mind is that it will give me a chance to get to know John and Marie a bit better. While we have worked in the same unit, we never have had an opportunity to get to know each other all that well. I think I will like and enjoy that.*

Karen: *Yes, that does sound like a positive for you. Is there anything else?*

Georgina: *Well, yes. I have never had an opportunity to try out new ideas with my peers. I think it will allow me to experiment without risking any damage to my relationship with the customer.*

Karen: *Yes, I can see where that would be a plus as well. Is there anything else you can think of?*

Georgina: *Well, the third thing that comes to me as we talk about it is that I will get the opportunity to benefit from all of John and Marie's experience. They have been around a lot of years and have worked with a lot of customers. I am sure I will learn something from the two of them.*

Karen: *Wow, that's a lot of good stuff. I am getting excited for you just listening to it all. Keep me posted as to how it is going.*

Summary: Restructuring Cycle Options Phase

Second phase of the Restructuring Cycle, which includes four phases: Identification, Options, Practice, and Habituation.

The purpose of the Options Phase is fourfold:

1. To help an individual clarify their desired outcomes

2. To identify and own their thinking and behavior

3. To generate as many alternatives as possible

4. To recognize the Pay Value that may come from a change in behavior

Options Phase fosters and supports creative thinking to generate many possibilities

Goals for the Options Phase

1. Clarify and have employee own their intentionality

2. Have employee recognize counter-intentional thoughts and resulting behavior

3. Guide employee to generate alternatives to current state

4. Help employee to identify Pay Value that will come from change

    *   Doing Pay Values which come from the process of change

    *   Being Pay Values which come from successfully achieving the new state

Behavior is not wrong, but rather counter-intentional

11

Practice and Habituation Phases of the Restructuring Cycle

With her options clearly defined, Georgina is ready to start practicing new behaviors.

Practice Phase

Her coaches, John and Marie, will provide a safe environment where she can experiment, refine, and perfect her new approaches. John and Marie, along with Karen, will have to provide role models for Georgina. Most of us recognize the importance of providing positive role models. These role models present a set of behavioral routines to emulate. They present the "do it like this" model. But it is equally important to present negative role models as well. Most people, when presented with a new set of behaviors, don't copy them exactly. They naturally superimpose their own style and personality over those behaviors presented by the positive role model. Sometimes, with that adaptation, they deviate to the point that they alter the behavior in a negative way. Negative role models help set the boundaries of what is acceptable and what is not. They provide the outer limits for that personal adaptation.

Karen should also, at this point, arrange to have some peer support for Georgina. She needs to get the rest of the service team involved in providing positive feedback and constructive suggestions to Georgina.

Habituation Phase

The Habituation Phase begins once Georgina has reached the point with her practice that she is ready to try the new behaviors in her real world work setting. Any new behavior feels awkward when an individual first starts to use it. As one performs it over and over again, the behavior becomes second nature. As it becomes habitual, a manager's role becomes to help the employee identify successes and to provide positive reinforcement for the new routine.

Summary: Restructuring Cycle Practice and Habituation Phases

Third and Fourth phases of the cognitive Restructuring Cycle, which includes four phases: Identification, Options, Practice, and Habituation.

Practice Phase

- Provide safe environment for employee's new behavior
- Furnish role models for new behavior
- Structure peer support for behavioral change

Habituation Phase

- Perform new behavior in normal work routine
- Manager helps identify success
- Provide positive reinforcement to strengthen new behavior

Summary: Restructuring Cycle

Targets for Restructuring

- Perfectionism
- Catastrophizing
- Fairness Fallacy
- Blaming
- Polarized Thinking

Identification Phase

- What is the individual thinking?
- What is the individual feeling?
- What is the individual doing?
- Are there counter-intentional thoughts, feelings, or behaviors?

Options Phase

- Clarify and create ownership for individual's intentionally
- Help the individual recognize the counter-intentional thought and the counter-intentional behavior that results.
- Guide the individual as s/he researches and develops alternatives
- Help the individual identify the Pay Value to modifying their thoughts and behavior.

Practice Phase

- Provide coaches to create a safe environment
- Provide positive and negative role models—do it like this, don't do it like that
- Provide peer support and feedback

Habituation Phase

- Help identify successes and provide positive reinforcement
- Remember, that a failure you learn from is also a success

12

Envisioning the Future

Another useful tool to help an individual tap into his or her own motivation is Envisioning the Future. This tool is a structured probing process designed to help someone figure out where their current behavior might take them. It answers the question "What is this probably leading me towards?"

The most difficult part of the process is having the patience to allow the individual to work through it for him or her self. Envisioning the Future takes a great deal of patience and time. You can't force feed it.

Case Study: Fred's Reason For Working

Fred's case presents a common situation that serves as a good example. He was a young man, still living at home with his parents. He was working in an entry-level position; the kind people typically refer to as grunt work. His commitment and engagement with the work were tenuous at best. Fred was chronically late coming to work. This behavior was driving Mack, Fred's supervisor, to distraction. When Fred was there, his performance was acceptable, but his tardiness was very frustrating to Mack. Under other circumstances, Mack might have just fired Fred. But Mack was operating in a very tight labor market. He knew that it would not be easy to find a replacement for Fred so he was committed to trying to work with him to change this one undesirable behavior.

While working with a group of manager's that included Mack, he raised the lateness issue with Fred as a case study. The group decided to help Mack work through this situation and decided to try Envisioning the Future as the first step towards supporting Fred's positive behavioral change. Envisioning the Future involves four phases:

1. What do you want?

2. What are you getting?

3. What direction are you moving?

4. What changes do you want to make?

What Do You Want?

The first phase in Envisioning the Future is to help the individual figure out what it is they want out of a situation, interaction, or set of circumstances. So the peer-coaching group guided Mack to start there. When Mack said he was willing to try the process, he didn't know what he was letting himself in for.

Since the problem with Fred involved him coming late to work, the group decided Mack should start by trying to help Fred figure out why he wanted to come to work at all. Little did Mack realize that this simple question would test his creativity and patience.

Let's listen in to Mack's first conversation with Fred.

Mack: *Fred, you know I've talked with you several times before about being late all the time. I want to talk with you about that again. It is still a problem and I want to learn more about what's going on with you. In thinking about this, I realized I didn't know much about your situation or what you want from this job. Why do you come to work at all?*

Fred: *Well, because you pay me and I need the money.*

Mack: *That makes sense. I guess to some degree that's true for all of us. In addition to that (the needing the money) why else do you come to work?*

Fred: *Well, I live with my mom and dad. My mom says that I need to get out of the house and earn some money. She says I can't just lay around and watch TV all day and play computer games. So, I guess it's because she makes me work. If I don't she'll probably throw me out of the house.*

Mack: *So you work to get the money and because your Mom makes you.*

Fred: *Yea.*

Mack: *Is there anything else?*

Fred: *No, I guess that's about it.*

Now Mack could, at this point, use power and control to plant the idea that Fred's current behavior might lead to him losing his job (a Fear Vector). But, in a tight labor market, the chances are good that Fred knows he can get another grunt job to keep his Mom off his back. So that Fear Vector will probably not be effective. Mack, with some coaching from his peer-group, decided to take a different track. Let's see where he takes it.

Mack: *So are you telling me Fred, that if your Mom would let you, you would stay home all day and watch TV and play computer games?*

Fred: *Yea, I would love that.*

Mack: *Have you ever done that for a long time? Like on the weekend or something?*

Fred: *Yea, when we were on vacation last year, before I came to work here I did it all the time.*

Mack: *How long was the vacation?*

Fred: *A week.*

Mack: *Did you watch TV and play games the whole week?*

Fred: *No, after about 3 days of that, I got tired of it and we did some other stuff.*

Mack: *So are you telling me that even if your mother didn't force you to work and you could stay home and watch TV and play computer games that, after a while, you would get tired of it?*

Fred: *Yea, Sure!*

Mack: *Well suppose we were at that point. You were tired of staying home and bored with watching TV and playing games and you decided to come back into work. What would make you want to do that?*

Fred: *Well…(starting to answer)*

Mack: *No, Fred. I don't want you to answer me right now. I want you to think about it for a couple of days and we'll talk again on Thursday. Don't answer me now. Think about it. If you had the choice about whether to work or not, why would you choose to come in?*

Fred: *Okay.*

Notice that Mack didn't let Fred come up with a quick, easy answer. He wants Fred to think about it. Let's analyze this situation in terms of the Motivational Vector Grid, represented by **Fig. 12.1**.

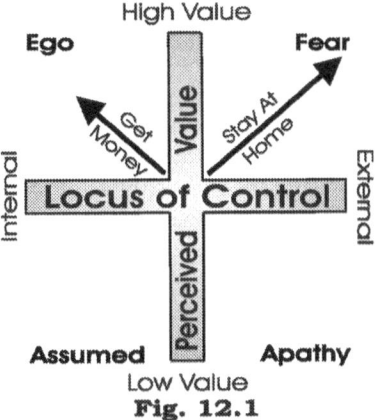

Fig. 12.1

Right now, Fred has talked about two vectors: needing money and the pressure he is feeling from his mother. For the money, it is something he values (although not enough to worry about the value of the money he loses when his pay is docked for coming in late). It is also something that is in his Locus of Control. He controls how much time he devotes to earning money (as witnessed by his choice to be late frequently). So that Motivational Vector is in the Ego category. There is also the pressure he is feeling from mom to have a job or be thrown out of the house. Living in the house seems to be something he values and it is out of his control, so that Motivational Vector is in the Fear Quadrant.

What Mack is trying to help Fred uncover is another Pay Value. The very essence of Envisioning the Future is to try to help an individual uncover and/or clarify what they want. Let's hear what happens when Mack talks to Fred on Thursday.

Mack: *Well Fred, have you come up with other things that make you want to come to work, I mean, in addition to the money and the fact that your Mom forces you to?*

Fred: *Yea, I thought about it quite a bit. I never really thought about it like that before, so it was hard for me. But there is one thing I came up with.*

Mack: *Yes, what's that?*

Fred: *Believe it or not, I really like interacting with all the other folks on my team here. I like the way we joke around on breaks and I like the way people pay attention to me.*

Mack: *So you like being part of the team?*

Fred: *Yea.*

Now Mack has something to work with. It took him two interactions with Fred over three days, but he has helped Fred identify something else that he wants from work. Now Mack can move on to the next phase.

What Are You Getting?

So Mack can now guide Fred to explore the results he is getting from his current behavior and how it relates to his desire to be part of the team.

Mack: *Fred let me ask you, if you want to be part of the team, do you ever wonder what the rest of the team think of you as a team member, I mean?*

Fred: *Well, no, I always kind of took it for granted that if I worked with them, then I was part of the team.*

Mack: *Would you like to find out?*

Fred: *Yea, I suppose I would.*

Mack: *Suppose you take the next three days and talk with the other members of the team to find out what they think about you as a team member? We can get back together next Wednesday to see what you have found out.*

Fred: *Okay.*

So now, Mack has set the stage for Fred to answer the question "where am I now?" in relation to his goal of being a team member.

Notice how Mack makes every effort to keep the Locus of Control internal to Fred. Since they are talking about something Fred has said is important to him, Mack is trying to keep the Motivational Vector in the Ego Quadrant.

What Direction Are You Moving?

Let's see what Fred has discovered in talking with the rest of his team.

Mack: *So Fred, what did you find out about how the other team members view you?*

Fred: *Well, it's pretty bad. They pretty much think I am a slug and a screw-up. The only thing good I heard is that I'm funny.*

Mack: *You say it like being funny isn't a good thing. I love funny people. What's wrong with funny?*

Fred: *Well, there's funny and then there's funny. Sometimes funny is good, like a comedian is funny and that's great. But I got the feeling that they meant funny like screw-up kind of funny, like you laugh when somebody does or says something stupid.*

Mack: *Oh, I see. When you put it like that it doesn't seem too good to me either.*

Fred: *Yea, I don't want to be the screw-up to get laughs.*

Mack: *Well what are some of the other words you heard that describe you?*

Fred: *Undependable is one. A lot of people said they couldn't count on me. Others said I was a goof-off. One even said I was a loser!*

Mack: *Wow, Fred, that's tough to hear. Let me ask you this, is that what you wanted people to think about you?*

Fred: *Heck no! I mean, I know I haven't been too serious about the job, but I didn't think I was that bad!*

Mack: *Yea, I hear ya. It's tough to hear that kind of stuff from anybody, particularly folks you want to interact with everyday. What kind of words would you like them to use to describe you, Fred?*

Fred: *Well, I'd like to be thought of as smart, dependable, and someone you could count on.*

Mack: *So what you're doing now isn't giving you the reaction you want, is it?*

Fred: *No, definitely not!*

Mack: *One of the rules they taught me in a training program is that if what you are doing now isn't working, anything else is better. Do you want to make a change, Fred? Or, do you want to keep going the direction you're going here?*

Fred: *I want to make a change. I can't be part of the team with people thinking of me like that!*

Now Mack has led Fred right up to the edge of the next phase. He has helped Fred identify the gap between the results he wants and the results he is getting. He has also helped him make a choice to try something different.

What Changes Do You Want To Make?

A common managerial response when an employee says they want to make a change is for the manager to start making suggestions about things that they should change. But Mack isn't going to go there with Fred. He understands the Motivational Vector Grid and is going to keep the Locus of Control in the Internal range, that is, with Fred.

Mack: *At this point Fred I'm suggesting that you think about this some more. You've identified some words that you associate with the kind of team member you want to be: smart, dependable, and someone you could count on. Why don't you think about how someone who you would describe with those words would act? Then we can get back together on Friday and see what you've come up with that you might want to change.*

Fred: *I know what I need to change now!*

Mack: *I'm sure you have some ideas now. What I would like you to do is think about those and also be thinking about which one is most important to you. That way you can decide which one you want to work on first. Does that make sense to you?*

Fred: *Yea. I guess it would make sense to think about it.*

Now when Mack and Fred get back together Mack can help him prioritize what change he wants to work on first. This approach will help Fred and assure that he doesn't get overwhelmed.

Summary: Envisioning the Future

Envisioning the future is a structured probing process designed to help someone figure out where their current behavior might take them

The process requires patience to allow the employee to work through it

There are four phases to Envisioning the Future

1. What do you want?
2. What are you getting?
3. What direction are you moving?
4. What changes do you want to make?

Manager should keep Locus of Control with Employee

13

Probing Cycle

The Probing Cycle is a three part structured approach to asking questions designed to help an employee deeply examine their behavior. More than any other skill, a manager working with an employee using the Motivational Vector Grid needs good probing skills. There is a tendency for managers to rush the process to get the employee working immediately on a solution. This penchant for action, while it may be satisfying emotionally for a manager seldom leads to lasting behavioral change for the employee.

In working with managers and supervisors, I have found that it helps to fit this skill into a structured probing cycle. This helps the manager keep the Locus of Control well within the employee's range and also helps uncover what Pay Value the employee holds the highest.

The Probing Cycle goes through three phases:

1. Assessment

2. Gap Analysis

3. Action Planning and Prioritization

Assessment Phase

During the Assessment Phase, a manager's probes should be geared towards establishing what the individual knows or is aware of. It is the phase where you try to figure out how the current behavior became established as routine.

Typically, behavior is formed because a particular behavioral routine, at some time, produced a desired result or emotional state. In other words, we do something or act a certain way because it achieved a satisfying outcome in the past. This is a useful approach that helps people establish habitual routines that are functional in their lives. It only causes difficulty when the situation changes and the behavior remains the same. In other words, an individual continues to do something even though it no longer produces the desired result.

It is often said that people don't like to change. One of the reasons that this statement has the ring of truth to it is because people tend to resist change that calls for them to change established routines that have produced desired results for them in the past. If you ever hope to help someone motivate him or herself to change, you have to help them evaluate the circumstances and conditions under which they established their current behavior. Then help them examine the current conditions and circumstance to decide if enough of a change has occurred to have them make a choice to change to a new routine. Your probes should address the specifics of when they first started the behavioral routine in question and what happened at the time to make that behavioral response seem like the best option.

The pattern for this Assessment Phase is:

1. Describe the behavioral routine and acknowledge efficacy

2. Probe to determine other successful instances of the behavior

3. Probe to determine the current circumstances and conditions of use

Case Study: Yvonne's Angry Outbursts

Darnell's situation with Yvonne is a good example of phase one of the Probing Cycle. Yvonne works on a team of six people that must cooperate closely to provide service to their customers. Yvonne has been with the team almost a year and her technical skills are excellent. However, she has demonstrated a tendency to have angry outbursts with other team members when the team is operating under tight deadlines. Several of her team members have complained to Darnell. This has only happened, so far, in the team environment. Yvonne has never had an outburst when the team is with a customer, but Darnell is concerned that the pattern may get worse and wants to nip it in the bud. Let's listen in as he meets with Yvonne.

Darnell: *Yvonne, you have excellent technical skills and I have been very pleased with the quality and quantity of your technical performance. You know our products and services and it shows in the contribution you make to our team. Your ability to help the team meet deadlines contributes to our overall success. Today I want to talk about a behavioral pattern that I observed last week. Last Thursday, when we were all working on meeting that deadline for Acme Services, you had, what seemed to me, an angry outburst. You raised your voice well above a conversational level, made personal attacks on other team members, and even appeared physically aggressive, leaning in towards Fred as you yelled at him and waved your arms above your head. In fact, I saw this same pattern repeat itself several times during the day. It seemed quite routine for you. I'm curious. Has this behavior helped you meet deadlines in the past?*

Yvonne: *I know I tend to come on pretty strong when I am pushing to meet a deadline. I might have seemed angry, but it's just my way of being forceful. I find that it makes people respond to my requests faster.*

Darnell: *Can you give me some examples of other times when using that forceful approach has been successful for you?*

Yvonne: *Well, last month when we were facing that tight deadline for the Martek account and Sue and Barry were dragging their feet on their part I used it very successfully. I hollered a bit and leaned over them and they soon got on the stick.*

Darnell: *So you've found that behavioral approach successful in many instances?*

Yvonne: *Well, yes. I've used it as long as I can remember. It gets things moving. It might intimidate some folks, but they get over it.*

Darnell: *So, you see a lot of benefit to it and see few long-term downside con-sequences from it because people get over it quickly enough.*

Yvonne: *Yea. They don't take it personally. It's just business and we have to make those deadlines.*

So Yvonne is using a behavioral strategy (getting angry) because she has found that it worked for her in the past. In addition, she seems to feel that there have been few or no negative effects of using that behavioral strategy. She hasn't observed (or been made aware of) any problems that the strategy has caused her and her team members.

Gap Analysis Phase

The purpose of this phase is to help the individual identify changes in the environment that might call into question their current approach to the situation.

The pattern for this Gap Analysis Phase is:

1. Introduce new information about the situation or environment

2. Evaluate the value and implication of the new information

3. Solicit a conclusion

Let's listen in as Darnell works through this Gap Analysis Phase with Yvonne.

Darnell: *Well, Yvonne, it sounds like you've developed a system that really works for you.*

Yvonne: *Yea, it seems to give me the results I want.*

Darnell: *I have some information that I would like to share with you that might be important. I've had five complaints from your co-workers that they feel your approach is too aggressive and that they would like to have you re-assigned to another team. I know you are thinking that your co-workers understand your need to use this behavior and that they will get over it, but it seems that they are feeling quite differently.*

Yvonne: *God, why didn't they say something to me instead of running to you behind my back! With all that I contribute to the team, I can't believe they'd undermine me like this.*

Darnell: *Actually, I was curious about that myself and ask them why they didn't say something to you. They all said they simply weren't comfortable in talking with you about it because they felt you might just react with another angry outburst.*

Yvonne: *Wow! Afraid to talk to me? I've always thought of myself as easy to talk to. Don't they know it's just the way I am under pressure? I don't mean anything personal by it.*

Darnell: *A couple of folks mentioned your tendency to make personal attacks specifically. Apparently, people do take the name calling personally; even if it is just something that comes out in the heat of the moment.*

Yvonne: *I didn't realize they were so sensitive.*

Darnell: *In fact, I am concerned myself because it seems like this pattern is getting worse and I am concerned that it will spill over to your interaction with our customers.*

Yvonne: *I would never be like that with a customer. Have you had any complaints?*

Darnell: *No, and I don't want any. By they way, the other members of the team are internal customers. Perhaps you shouldn't have a different standard for those internal customers.*

Yvonne: *Well, I expect my team members to understand.*

Darnell: *Obviously, some of them don't understand. They are offended and concerned about your behavior.*

Yvonne: *Yes, I hear that.*

Darnell: *Now that you know that, what value do you find in that information?*

Yvonne: *Well, I don't want people not wanting to work with me. I'm glad I know how they feel. I had no idea I was upsetting people to that extent.*

Darnell: *Well, if this continues what do you think is going to happen?*

Yvonne: *I suppose you'll have to transfer me to another team.*

Darnell: *Do you want that?*

Yvonne: *No, I don't.*

Darnell: *What do you think should happen now?*

Yvonne: *Well, I guess I better make a change, and fast.*

Darnell has helped Yvonne see that she needs to make a change. The new information he presented her caused Yvonne to examine her assumptions about the environments and realize that something was qualitatively different. Her original operating assumptions were off base. Yvonne is now ready for the last phase.

Action Planning and Prioritization Phase

In this phase, Darnell will help Yvonne list specific steps that she will take to improve her ability to interact with people without resorting to anger. Her Action Plan will list, in addition to the actions she will take, the resources, timeframes, and collaboration that will occur.

Summary: The Probing Cycle

The Probing Cycle is a three part structured approach to asking questions designed to help an employee deeply examine their behavior.

The Probing Cycle goes through three phases:

1. Assessment

   - Establish what the employee knows or is aware of

   - Determine how current behavior was established as routine

     - Describe the behavioral routine and acknowledge efficacy

     - Probe to determine other successful instances of the behavior

     - Probe to determine the current circumstances and conditions of use

2. Gap Analysis

   - Manager introduces new information about the situation or environment

   - Employee evaluates the value and implication of the new information

   - Manager solicits a conclusion from employee about the need for change

3. Action Planning and Prioritization

   - Employee creates a list of tasks, noting resources, timeframes, and collaboration needed

14

Feedback Cycle

By this time if you've used the tools and approaches that you've learned in this book the person you are coaching has established the new, desired behavioral routine. To assure continued progress you must provide feedback that is both timely and comprehensive.

Here are some basic guidelines to timing feedback. When a behavior is new to an individual and not well established, your feedback should be given regularly. The further the desired new behavior is from established behavioral routines the more frequent your feedback should be.

Think of a parent's frequency of feedback when a child is learning to walk. The parent pays constant attention to any movement that is even vaguely related to walking. When they see the desired behavior they provide immediate and effusive feedback. "*Come on sweetie, get your steady.*"

While the people you'll be working with are not young children, the principle is exactly the same. The more novel and foreign the behavior; the more frequently and enthusiastically it needs to be reinforced.

As the new desired behavior becomes established, your feedback can be spaced at longer intervals. Eventually, your feedback need only be periodic and random to maintain the desired behavior.

Look Back, Look Around, Look Forward

One technique that helps ensure that your feedback is comprehensive is the *Look Back, Look Around, Look Forward* technique. As the name implies, this technique provides feedback on what has happened in the past, what is currently happening, and what (if current behavior continues) may occur in the future.

In preparation for providing feedback using the *Look Back, Look Around, Look Forward* technique, it is useful to review any Motivational Vector Grids and notes that you have created in working towards the desired behavioral change.

Look Back

First, when providing feedback on past performance do not dwell on the undesirable behavior that has been changed. You should, however, review the circumstances and conditions that led to the need for behavioral change. This review serves to resell the individual on their decision to change.

Second, it is also important to review and reinforce all the effort that the employee has put forth to establish their new behavioral routine. If that effort has led to positive change, provide praise. If the effort resulted in unsuccessful outcomes, stress the learning that has occurred. This allows the individual to understand that no effort is wasted if they learned from it. It will be useful to refer to the Action Plan the individual created as their roadmap for change.

The last step in the *Look Back* step is to reinforce any positive Pay Value the individual may have experienced from their behavioral change. If they are relating better to coworkers, being more productive, or feeling more comfortable in their work, make certain that you acknowledge the benefit they have received from their new behavior.

Look Around

After the *Look Back*, you can then move to *Look Around* to provide feedback on the employee's current performance. Include data on any performance measures that were agreed upon as benchmarks for successful behavioral change. Also solicit the individual's input on the support you have been providing in helping them change their behavior.

Look Forward

It may seem odd to include *Look Forward* during a feedback session. After all isn't feedback, by its very nature, only related to events that have already occurred? Following a strict dictionary definition of the word *then Look Forward* should not be included in feedback. However, we are not trying to write a dictionary. We are trying to provide feedback that will support and encourage new behavior.

First, to prepare for the *Look Forward*, evaluate the unfinished portion of the Action Plan. Action Plans are living documents that must be revised and amended to reflect the current reality.

Second, review organizational conditions and requirements that make the new behavior necessary. Keep in mind you must be constantly selling the need for, and benefits of the new behavior.

Finally, express your confidence that the individual can continue their success pattern in changing behavior. It is critical to always end your feedback session with a positive expectancy for the future.

Case Study: Gerald Adapts to New Management

Gerald makes a good case study to illustrate this technique in action. To set the stage, we'll go through Gerald's situation in detail. This will not only give the reader necessary background to understand Look Back, Look Around, Look Forward, it will also illustrate how to integrate some of the other tools while working with an employee.

Nine months ago there was a significant change in the organizational structure. Gerald had performed mostly analytical functions where he could work alone. He published his results in well thought out, polished documents. He had always been considered a reliable high performer and was well respected by his colleagues. Then Gerald's work environment transitioned to a team-oriented, matrix management structure. The change required Gerald to communicate face-to-face with team members on a regular basis. Early in the transition, his supervisor, Janet, received several complaints about Gerald's ability to communicate face-to-face. It became painfully obvious to her that Gerald would need to make drastic improvements to his interpersonal communication skills. Janet has been working with Gerald for six months to improve his performance in that area.

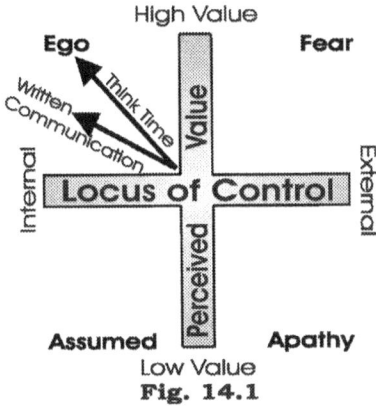

Fig. 14.1

Janet's first step was to create an initial Motivational Vector Grid to give her a starting point for coaching Gerald, as illustrated in **Fig. 14.1**. In working with Gerald before the change, Janet knew that he liked to have time to think about his work, research his approach, and plan out his response when providing service to an internal customer. He called it his think time. Fortunately, the work environment allowed him sufficient time to follow this pattern. In addition, Gerald liked to communicate in writing because he felt he could be better organized and more comprehensive in his answers. It was also fortunate for Gerald that the environment allowed him to respond to his internal customers primarily in writing. In talking with Gerald, he made it clear that having the think time was most important to him and that being able to communicate in writing, was less important. Gerald felt like he could do okay communicating face-to-face as long as he had enough think time. Since Gerald's work environment allowed him both the think time and the time to communicate in writing, both were well in his Locus of Control.

Once Gerald was placed in the new environment and the complaints started, Janet met with Gerald to discuss the complaints. Here's what that sounded like:

Janet: *Gerald, you know that you've been a solid contributor in this company for a long time. Your attention to detail, thoughtful research, and well-constructed answers to others have gained you a lot of respect as an analyst.*

Gerald: *I'm glad to hear you say that Janet. Here lately I've been feeling like things have changed drastically. I used to be able to take the time I needed to research and construct my answers. Now, everyone wants me to participate in these team meetings and give them an answer on the fly as soon as something comes up. I don't do well like that. It makes me feel uncertain of myself and the work that I do.*

Janet: *Yes the environment has changed. As you know, the new president is trying to implement a different management style. He calls it matrix team-oriented management. It really has changed the way we work.*

Gerald: *I'll say! I don't like it one bit. Now it seems like I am always having to make excuses about why I need more time to respond to requests. People get mad with me and rush me. Then I feel like I give them a faulty product and it makes me feel like I am not doing a good job. Why can't we just do it like we did before? That worked very well for me.*

Notice that Janet started from a strengths perspective, reviewing those preferences that had previously earned Gerald the respect of his co-workers. However, in the new environment, Janet knows she must help Gerald accept and embrace this change. But before moving forward with him, she takes a minute to take stock of how this situation is impacting Gerald's Motivational Vector Grid.

She mentally revises Gerald's Motivational Vector Grid. Hearing what he has to say and realizing that he still values his think time and written communication style, but that he feels like it is no longer in his control, his Motivational Vector Grid now looks like **Fig. 14.2**.

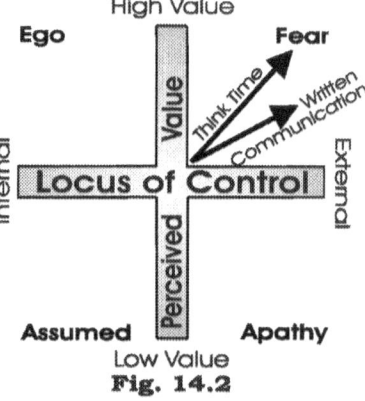

Fig. 14.2

At this point, Gerald's Motivational Vector has moved from the Ego Quadrant to the Fear Quadrant. He is feeling out of control. He is longing for days gone by and the way things use to be. His anxiety is high and he probably is going to be resistant to any changes that Janet might suggest.

Janet mentally evaluates her tool set and decides to use the Probing Cycle with Gerald.

Let's listen in as she directs the conversation to step one, the Assessment Phase of the Probing Cycle.

Janet: *Gerald, how long have you been using your thoughtful approach to producing results?*

Gerald: *I've been using the same approach for almost five years.*

Janet: *I'm curious, what happened that led you to develop your approach? What led you to try it in the first place?*

Gerald: *Well, about six months after I was put in this job, Harry Anderson was working on a big account and came to me to ask for help. He had been working with Suzanne, but the client wasn't pleased with her work. Harry was dealing with the CFO who is really detail oriented and liked to see a lot of background information before making a decision. When Harry explained that to me, it just seemed like a good idea to take think time and produce something well organized and well written. When Harry used my report with the client they were thrilled. They are still one of our largest accounts today. My manager at the time gave me a bonus, wrote an article about me in the newsletter, and held me up as a positive example to the rest of my team. Ever since then, I've been using the same approach. And it worked just fine till this change hit me.*

Janet: *Can you give me some examples of other accounts that we've won and kept because of your good work?*

Gerald: *Yes, the Antec account, the Maple City account, and the Jones-Hennesy account are all, at least partially, a result of my work.*

Janet: *Well, it's no wonder you are frustrated by the change. The approach you have been using has been successful for both you and the company in the past.*

Gerald: *Yes, that's why I'm having such a hard time with the change.*

Now, Janet has finished the assessment phase of the Probing Cycle and is ready to move into the gap analysis. Let's listen in as she moves forward with Gerald.

Janet: *Gerald, you mentioned that you feel like things have changed. Can you elaborate on that? Tell me more about how you feel things have changed.*

Gerald: *It seems like everything has changed to me. Nothing is like it used to be!*

Janet: *I know it seems like that to you but can you be more specific.*

Gerald: *Well now I have to get to a lot more face-to-face meetings. People expect me to give them data on the fly. I seem to be involved in many more projects then I use to be. And, I'm interacting with a whole lot more people than I use to. Many of them don't know me, and I don't know them.*

Janet: *Do you think these changes only happened in your work or have there been changes to the work situations of others as well?*

Gerald: *It seems like the whole company has changed! The new president has remade us into something that I don't even recognize.*

Janet: *Do you have any idea what prompted him to make these changes?*

Gerald: *I think so. I know that other companies have moved into the market and are competing very aggressively with us. I know that has been a strain on our profits and our growth.*

Janet: *Do you know any of the particulars about how those new companies are competing with us?*

Gerald: *Yes, I'm friends with Annie in sales. She says that not only do they charge less, but also they respond faster to customer requests.*

Janet: *Can you relate that change in competition to the changes that the new president has made to the way we work?*

Gerald: *Well, it certainly makes sense that we would all have to move faster to make certain that we can respond at least as quickly as the competition.*

Janet: *Are you also aware that teams under our new structure are supporting a twenty-five percent larger customer base than the same people were under the old structure?*

Gerald: *Wow, twenty-five percent more? That's a big jump.*

Janet: *How do you suppose that increase in productivity affects our ability to respond to price pressures from our competition?*

Gerald: *It's got to help.*

Janet: *Yes, if our projections are correct, it will mean a fifteen-percent growth rate for us this year.*

Gerald: *Fifteen percent! That's more than we've ever done since I've been here.*

Janet: *That's why the new management has made the changes and why I need you to work diligently to make this new arrangement a success. So now that we've reviewed all these changes and their potential impact, what conclusions can you draw about what you need to do from here?*

Gerald: *Well, it sounds like I need to make some changes.*

Now, Janet has the commitment she needs to move into the third phase of the Probing Cycle—Action Planning and Prioritization.

Let's listen in again as she moves forward with Gerald.

Janet: *OK Gerald, if you want to change let's see if we can come up with some specific steps that you can take to make this change successful for you and the company. What type of things do you think you should be doing to facilitate the change?*

Gerald: *Well, in the past I have relied heavily on printed resources to do my research. I have cabinets filled with data and reports. While this information is useful, it takes me a lot of time to find what I need each time I do some research. Most of that information is now available through online databases. If we could get subscriptions to the two main databases, it would substantially speed up the research process. In fact, if I had a laptop with a wireless connection, I could do some of that research on the fly right in the meetings.*

Janet: *OK that's great. Can you give me a one-page summary by the end of the week that outlines the costs and the technical requirements to set up those databases for you?*

Gerald: *Sure.*

Janet: *Thanks. That will help with the research part. What about the writing?*

Gerald: *Well, there are two things I can think of. First, I can create some templates and stock paragraphs in Word. That will give me a jump on any writing I have to do. Second, I can probably focus my work more clearly by asking questions of the rest of the team to make sure I'm not giving them more than they need. This will probably cut back on the amount of writing I have to do.*

Janet: *That is a great idea, Gerald. That, combined with the database assess should really help. Let's put both of them down in writing in an Action Plan right now (taking up a piece of paper to write).*

Gerald: *Yes, I can implement both of those in the next seven days.*

Janet: *That's great. One other thing we need to think about, however, is how to help you better manage your personal relationships with the members of the team.*

Gerald: *Don't you think that the things we've talked about already will help that?*

Janet: *Yes, I do, and I'm excited to see the results as you put them into practice. However, I think these changes will only get us part of the way to where we need to be. You see the feedback I had from others on the team concerns not only the technical work you do for them but also how you interact with them. I would like you to consider exposing yourself to some information on personal styles and how they affect interpersonal relationships at work. Last year, I participated in a workshop on personal styles and I found it very useful. The same company is conducting another one next month. Would you consider attending that as part of your Action Plan?*

Gerald: *I don't know. I hate all that touchy-feely stuff. It just seems dumb to me.*

Janet: *I have some sense of what you mean. That is sort of the way I felt when I attended. Actually, my boss forced me to attend. I hated him for it at the time, but I have to admit that I have found it very useful. I don't want to force you to go, so how about this. Next Friday, I'll review my workshop materials with you and share with you some of the ways I have put this information to use. After we do that, you can decide if you want to go. If you decide not to go, it will be up to you to come up with at least two action items that we can agree on to help you improve your interpersonal skills. Does that sound fair enough?*

Gerald: *So, you're not going to force me to go?*

Janet: *No, I'm not going to force you. I think you are intelligent and motivated. You can make up your own mind and choose something that will suit you.*

Gerald: *That's great!*

Janet: *Okay then I'll see you next Friday.*

Gerald: *Great, see you then.*

Note how positive and affirming Janet's interaction is with Gerald. She builds his sense of self-efficacy. Most important, her approach helped Gerald move his Motivational Vector from an external Locus of Control back to an internal Locus of Control. This moves his Motivational Vector from the Fear Quadrant back to the Ego Quadrant as illustrated in **Fig. 14.3**.

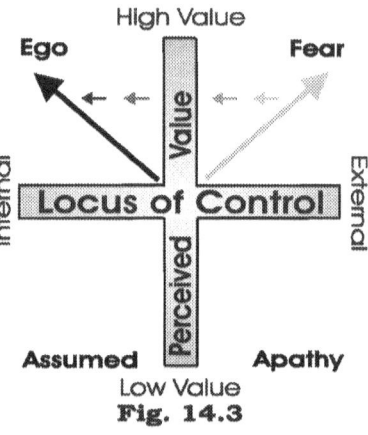

Fig. 14.3

From her conversation with Gerald, however, Janet realizes that she still faces a challenge about his feelings towards improving his interpersonal skills. His remark about hating touchy-feely stuff was a big caution sign to her. She knows she will need to help him re-think his position about that subject. Looking in her toolbox, she realizes this is a perfect opportunity to use the Restructuring Cycle. To prepare for her next meeting with Gerald on Friday she reviews that tool. Let's fast forward to that meeting and listen to how Janet puts the tool to work with Gerald.

Janet: *Good morning, Gerald. Before we review the workshop materials, I would like to take a minute to catch up with you and get an idea of how you are coming along on your Action Plan.*

Gerald: *Fantastic! I'm actually ahead of schedule. Here is the summary for the databases that you asked me to put together. I have a one-page summary that you asked for and I also added two pages behind that of some details you may need for budgeting purposes. I laughed at myself as I put those two pages together because I realized it was more than you asked me for, but I decided it may speed the process. I know how your boss likes details and I wanted you to have everything you need when you go in to ask for the money to support the database installation.*

Janet: *Well, the fact that you thought about it first shows a strong self-awareness and is a very positive thing. Also, I appreciate the thoughtfulness and have to agree that it will make my life easier as I budget the change. Thanks.*

Gerald: *No problem.*

Janet: *How are you coming with the templates and stock language?*

Gerald: *Great. The templates are done. I also shared them with some of the other folks on my team and Ken and Susan are also going to be using them. When I told them about the stock language idea, they got excited and volunteered to help with that if I would agree to share it. So we are developing that on the shared network drive so it will be available to all of us. Ken also told me about a software add-on to Word that might make it even easier. He is looking into that and will have something for us by the end of next week.*

Janet: *That's really great. It sounds like your excitement has rubbed off on some of the rest of the team. How does that feel for you?*

Gerald: *I haven't felt this good about what I am doing since the new president took over.*

Janet: *That's great, Gerald. I'm happy for you. Now let's take a look at that workshop material.*

Gerald: *Oh, I thought that with things going so well I wouldn't really need to do that.*

Janet: *That's interesting. Explain to me how you connect the way things have been going with your conclusion that you wouldn't need to work on your interpersonal skills.*

Gerald: *Well, I'm getting along well with my team members. The other folks are working with me on this thing. Everything is going fine. The problem is gone.*

Janet: *When you say, "the problem is gone," can you explain what problem you are referring to?*

Gerald: *The problem of my ability to get along with others. I am getting along.*

Janet: *So you are equating interpersonal skills with getting along with others?*

Gerald: *Isn't that what it means?*

Janet: *Well, that's part of it. But it also refers to your ability to communicate with others. It includes your ability to empathize with others and to appreciate and value their frame of reference, even when it is very different than yours. Interpersonal skills also include your ability to recognize and manage emotions—your own and others.*

Gerald: *But I am doing that now.*

Janet: *Yes, things are going well for you now. You are working with Ken and Susan on something you all agree is valuable. You also all agree on the priority and time frames involved. What happens when you are working with people that disagree about values, priorities, and time frames?*

Gerald: *I guess we'll all have to go to a class to learn how to share feelings and sing KumByYa around a campfire.*

Janet: *It sounds like you have very strong feelings about interpersonal skills training. Your description of singing around the campfire seems like it comes from very strong emotions. Talk to me some more about how you feel about that.*

Gerald: *Well, I went to some training a couple of years ago and they made me do some really stupid exercises with the other participants. At one point, we were put in groups and had to make up a song and sing it. I felt so stupid!*

Janet: *So you feel like all interpersonal skills training contains silly exercises that will make you feel stupid?*

Gerald: *Doesn't it?*

Janet: *Well, some of it does. I've been to workshops like you described and felt pretty much the way you did. If fact, the workshop I went to that we're going to review today had a few exercises like that. At first, I thought they were really silly and dumb, but the facilitator did a great job of showing me how those feelings I was having were a part of my own personal style. He helped me see the exercises from the frame of reference of some of the other people in the room. It helped me understand how their style was different than mine. Some of the exercises I enjoyed other people felt were stupid. Hearing what they had to say helped me understand even more.*

Gerald: *So you're saying that sometimes when I feel silly it's because of something to do with my personal style?*

Janet: *Sometimes, yes. It can be.*

Gerald: *I never thought of it that way.*

Janet: *Can you think of someone you always have difficulty interacting with or that you feel like you never quite get through to?*

Gerald: *Yes, Manny comes to mind immediately. He talks all the time and he is constantly changing his mind. He is always out in the stratosphere with his ideas and never seems to get down to brass tacks. It drives me crazy and makes it very difficult for me to work with him.*

Janet: *All of those characteristics you mentioned are related to Manny's personal style. If you get a better understanding of that style, it may make it easier for you to work with Manny.*

Gerald: *That would be a miracle!*

Janet has helped Gerald identify some counter-intentional thoughts related to interpersonal skills training. She has also helped Gerald identify and clarify what he is thinking, feeling, and doing. Now she is ready to move to the next phase of the Restructuring Cycle that will help Gerald identify options.

Janet: *How would it feel to you to be able to work more effectively with Manny?*

Gerald: *It would be fantastic. It would make my life at work much simpler and less stressful.*

Janet: *So you would find it valuable to improve your interpersonal skills if it could help you improve your ability to work with Manny and other folks that you find challenging or difficult now?*

Gerald: *Absolutely.*

Janet: *So you would like to work towards that, but you have some reservations about feeling uncomfortable in the classroom training?*

Gerald: *Yes, I would really like it if I could get the benefit without going through those silly and embarrassing exercises.*

Janet: *Can you think of any other ways you might learn the skills?*

Gerald: *I'm not sure. I can't think of anything right off the top of my head.*

Janet: *Well, think about when you have learned new skills in the past. How have you gone about that?*

Gerald: *That's a good question. Typically, I read a book. I also have used on-line training for some of the technical stuff.*

Janet: *Could you use that approach here?*

Gerald: *I don't know. I've never thought about it. I'm not sure what is available.*

Janet: *How could you find out?*

Gerald: *Well, I usually start with Amazon and the local library.*

Janet: *That sounds like a good start to me.*

At this point, Janet will give Gerald some time to work on researching available resources. She could have recommended some books or other resources, but she wanted to keep Gerald in the Internal Locus of Control.

Since he has some experience at learning new skills, she decided to let him demonstrate his self-efficacy.

Two weeks later, Janet has another session to continue the Restructuring Cycle with Gerald.

Janet: *I'm anxious to hear how you're progressing. What's gone on since the last time we talked?*

Gerald: *I am amazed how many books there are on the subject of interpersonal skills. I started in the library and never made it to Amazon because I found so much on the shelves.*

Janet: *Really, that's great. Have you settled on anything yet?*

Gerald: *The hard part was resisting the tendency to take out fifteen books at once. So what I decided to do is to skim several at the library, make a list of potential candidates, and then I talked with Marie, because I know she's into this stuff. I wanted to see if she knew anything about any of the books that seemed good to me.*

Janet: *Gerald, that was a great idea to use Marie as a resource. She is good at using interpersonal skills and seems to know how to flex her personal style to make working with others productive. Did she help you narrow your choices?*

Gerald: *Definitely. She recommended that I just use one book at a time. She went through my list with me and helped me choose one to start with.*

Janet: *Which book was it?*

Gerald: *Work Types—it's by a guy named Kroeger who is supposed to be really good at this stuff. I went to the library the same day and got it out. I am on my second reading of it now.*

Janet: *Are you finding it useful?*

Gerald: *Yes, definitely.*

Janet: *Did Marie have any other suggestions for you?*

Gerald: *Yes. She suggested that I have one person in mind as I read and that I try to apply what I read to my relationship with that person. I chose Manny because he was on my mind from our conversation.*

Janet: *That seems like a good suggestion. Let me ask you, Gerald, how would you feel about approaching Marie to act as your coach in this effort?*

Gerald: *A coach? What do you mean by that?*

Janet: *A coach is someone you can work with to practice the new skills you are trying to develop. They provide a safe test area so you can get use to the new behavioral pattern. Usually, when we first try something, it feels awkward or uncomfortable. Because of that discomfort, it is sometimes difficult to incorporate the new behavior into a day to day routine. The coach allows you to practice the behavior so you can get comfortable with it. That way, when you use it, it is like a pair of shoes that have been broken in. It's more comfortable.*

Gerald: *That makes sense. I'm going to ask her.*

Gerald is now well down the path to learning and incorporating a new set of behaviors into his day-to-day routines. Janet will monitor his progress and provide guidance to help Gerald celebrate his successes and see any setbacks as a learning experience.

Let's fast forward again. Now, after six months, Janet is ready to use the *Look Back, Look Around, Look Forward,* as part of her ongoing coaching with Gerald. Let's listen as Janet begins.

Janet: *Well, Gerald it has been six months since you made a decision to work an Action Plan to improve your interpersonal skills while working with the team. Let's take some time to look back at where you've come from, look around at how you're doing now, and then forward at the path you still have yet to travel.*

Gerald: *Okay.*

Janet: *You have always been a solid performer on the team. But six months ago we made the transition to a team-based matrix management environment that put new demands on you to interact with others in a way you were not accustomed to. This change highlighted the need for you to improve your ability to interact with others and sharpen your interpersonal skills.*

Gerald: *Yeah, that change was quite a shock to my world. I went from being a well-respected resource to a problem employee. I wasn't use to being thought of in that way.*

Janet: *And that dissatisfaction led you to develop and work on an Action Plan to improve your skills. I am impressed by the thought and work you have put in to your self-improvement process.*

Gerald: *Thanks, that's good to hear. It hasn't been easy and it was sometimes painful. I appreciate that you recognize my effort.*

Janet: *That effort has paid dividends. The number of negative comments I hear from your team members has fallen dramatically. In the last two weeks, I have only heard one piece of negative feedback. That was a comment from Margaret that you were short with her when she pressed you on a deadline. Also, in your last 360° survey, your results were up twenty percent higher than you were when you started. That is impressive progress.*

Gerald: *Thank you. It feels good to know that I'm heading in the right direction. I want to be thought of as a positive contributor to the team.*

Janet: *Your decision to use books as a resource seems to have worked well. You have been able to apply a great many of the approaches you've learned to your relationships with others you have had to work with. Even working with Manny has gotten easier for you, wouldn't you agree?*

Gerald: *Yes, the improvement in that relationship has been one of the major successes in this process for me. I can't say I like working with him, but it has gotten much less painful. The improvement is dramatic.*

Janet: *When we talked early on you said that improving your relationship with Manny would be a miracle. Has a miracle occurred?*

Gerald: *I don't know if there are degrees of miracles, but I would have to classify this as a minor miracle.*

Janet: *Great. I want you to know that I am also impressed by your decision to use Marie as a coach. I know that was a stretch for you to reach out and ask her for help. How is that working?*

Janet is now moving from the *Look Back* to the *Look Around* Phase. She has already given Gerald some hard data about the improvement he has made against their agreed on measures. But, she also wants to get some qualitative information.

Gerald: *Marie has been great. She is good at role-playing for me. Sometimes I have trouble not laughing because she is so good at playing Manny. Having the opportunity to practice a conversation with her before I actually have it with him has really helped.*

Janet: *That's great, Gerald. How about your reading program? How is that going?*

Gerald: *It's great. I'm in the middle of "Difficult Conversations" right now. It's a book about how to talk about the hard stuff with people. I am finding it very helpful.*

Janet: *That sounds like one I would enjoy reading myself. I'll have to put it on my reading list.*

Now, Janet can move on to the *Look Forward* phase.

Janet: *Well, it seems like you have completed all the items on your Action Plan and you are making excellent progress. How do you feel about it at this point?*

Gerald: *I am very pleased. I have to admit that when we first talked, I was kind of dreading this whole thing, but it has worked out well.*

Janet: *That's great that you've seen a benefit from it, Gerald. This change that has occurred in our organization has been challenging and you have definitely risen to that challenge. I am proud of all the work you have put into this.*

Gerald: *Thanks.*

Janet: *I still have a concern, however, about those situations where you have to speak extemporaneously to a group. You've made great progress in your one-on-one relationships, but the group speaking seems to still be a challenge for you.*

Gerald: *You're right. I hate doing that because I know I am not good at it. I do still need to work on that.*

Janet: *Have you given any thought to how you might best approach that?*

Gerald: *Unfortunately, it's not something that I think a book can help me with. I understand what the books say about it, but when I get up to talk none of that does me any good. I just freeze up and fumble and bumble through whatever I planned to say. It is very frustrating to me.*

Janet: *Is there anyone, like Marie, who might be able to help you with this?*

Gerald: *Not that I can think of.*

Janet: *Well, how might you come up with some Action Steps?*

Gerald: *I guess the same way I approach any other information need. I'll research.*

Janet: *Okay, where might you start that?*

Gerald: *The same place I start every research project, with Google.*

Now Gerald at least has a plan about how he is going to come up with a plan. Janet needs to continue to do Look Back, Look Around, Look Forward with Gerald on a periodic basis to make sure he feels supported.

Summary: Feedback Cycle

Guidelines for timing feedback
New behavior requires immediate and frequent feedback
The further the new behavior is from established routines, the more feedback needed

Look Back, Look Around, Look Forward: a technique that provides feedback on what has happened in the past, what is currently happening, and what (if current behavior continues) may occur in the future

Look Back

- Review Motivational Vector Grid and notes from previous meetings

- Focus on the change that has occurred, not the undesirable behavior from the past

- Review and reinforce all effort the employee has made

- Stress the learning that has occurred

- Reinforce any positive Pay Value from the change

Look Around

- Provide feedback on current performance

- Cite data from performance measures

- Solicit feedback on level and efficacy of management support

Look Forward

- Review and revise Action Plan

- Review organizational conditions and requirements that drove need for change

- Express confidence in employee's ability to continue a successful behavioral change

15

Applying the Framework, Tools, and Guides

Now, the next step is up to you. You've learned the framework represented by the Motivational Vector Grid. You've seen the guides on how to manage Perceived Value and Locus of Control. The tools and examples of how to use them have been presented. But nothing will change in your workplace unless you put what you've learned to work. Too often, we learn something but never apply it. Don't let that happen to what you've learned in this book.

If you're going to use what has been presented here, there are several actions you must take.

Start Today

The first and most obvious step is to start using the material right away. Sit down right now and begin working on an employee motivation problem. If you are in the fortunate position of not having an employee motivation problem right now, use one from the past.

Begin Using the Motivational Vector Grid

Start using the Motivational Vector Grid to analyze your own motivation for a particular situation. A good place to start is to complete a Motivational Vector Grid that shows the various forces that may act on your effort to use what you have learned in reading this book. Once you have decided which employee motivation problem to work on first, complete a Motivational Vector Grid for that employee. If you don't want to draw a blank motivational vector grid, go to www.personalalternatives.com/MIJ.htm and look for the *Download Tools* link to get a blank form to use.

Practice Using the Tools

You didn't walk upright the first time you tried. You fell down a lot before you got to the point where you were good at walking on two legs. The same thing will be true of your ability to use the tools in this book. You won't be good at using them the first time you try. You will need to practice.

It will be helpful for you to write a script of how you think it will go when you try to use the tool with your employee. It is a good idea to develop three or four scenarios that reflect how you think the employee will respond. It has been my experience that, if they think about it, a manager can develop three or four scenarios, one of which will accurately reflect how the employee will actually respond when the tool is used.

If you can do it without making the employee uncomfortable, record your interactions. That will allow you to review what you said and learn from each intervention. If you can't record an interaction, take the time to make detailed notes after each one. Remember that these notes are not to document what went on as part of some formal discipline process but to help you improve your ability to use new skills.

You may want to also attend one of our one-day workshops. This will provide a forum for you to deepen your understanding, practice your skills, and build a network of other people who are using this framework. Check the web site at www.personalalternatives.com for the schedule.

Don't Give Up

Too often I've seen a manager get frustrated while going through the learning curve to gain competence in using a new approach and simply give up. Don't let that happen to you. Keep practicing till you gain skill and confidence in using what you've learned.

Be Gentle With Yourself

As you apply your new skills, don't be too hard on yourself. If something is worth doing, it is worth doing badly to learn how to do it well. Don't beat up on yourself if you aren't perfect the first time you try. Make certain that you give yourself some positive feedback as you develop your ability. You may also want to ask the employees you interact with to provide some feedback about your approach.

Form a Peer-Coaching Network

The tools and guides presented here are social skills in the sense that they are about interacting with other people. One of the most powerful ways to sharpen your ability to use the framework, tools, and guides is to form a network with other people that are using it. This might be other people within your organization, or people that you meet through a local business organization such as the Chamber of Commerce. Even if you can only get together once a month it is very helpful to be able to present your motivational problem to others and to hear their suggestions and feedback. If you form a peer-coaching network, go to the web site to download the guide to presenting a case to a peer-coaching group.

http://www.personalalternatives.com/mij.htm.

If you can't form a local group, visit our web site to participate in the on-line discussion area.

Keep Learning

All of the tools and guides presented here have been field tested so I know they work. That doesn't mean they work for every employee and every motivation problem. Sometimes, even the tools presented here will not work with a particular motivation problem. That doesn't mean you give up. It simply means you need a bigger toolbox. Remember the Third Law of Motivational Vectors: *When they're stuck, it's your move.* So keep learning new techniques and approaches to expand the range of options you have in dealing with employee motivation problems.

Get To Work

Now it's time to close the book and get to work. Choose an employee motivation problem and start right now!

Index to the Framework, Guides, and Tools

The Framework

1.   Without outside intervention, the sum of the Motivational Vectors in any situation produces a stasis that will not change.

2.   In order to break stasis; an outside intervention must exert a force large enough to cause some significant change in direction or strength of an existing Motivational Vector.

3.   When they're stuck, it's always your move.

4.   If what you are doing now isn't working, anything else is better.

5.   The further away from the current Motivational Vector, the more motivational power is needed to create movement.

Guides Provided

4.   Applying the framework, guides, and tools   Chapter 15

Tools Presented

1.   Restructuring Cycle   Chapters 8–11

2.   Envisioning the Future   Chapter 12

3.   Probing Cycle   Chapter 13

4.   Feedback Cycle   Chapter 14

0-595-33948-4

www.ingramcontent.com/pod-product-compliance
Lightning Source LLC
Chambersburg PA
CBHW020245290526
45784CB00003B/1109